The
Hidden Zodiac

The
Hidden Zodiac

Sasha Fenton

A Sterling/Zambezi Book
Sterling Publishing Co., Inc
New York

Cover design: Jan Budkowski & Sasha Fenton
Illustrations & typesetting: Jan Budkowski
Editor: Julie Jones

Library of Congress Cataloging-in-Publication Data Available

Fenton, Sasha.
    The hidden zodiac : why you differ from others with your sun
sign / Sasha Fenton.
        p. cm.
    Includes index.
    ISBN 1-4027-0190-X
        1. Zodiac. 2. Individual differences–Miscellanea. I. Title.

BF1726 .F455 2002
133.5'2—dc21
                                                    2002066942

            2   4   6   8   10   9   7   5   3   1

        Published by Sterling Publishing Company, Inc.
        387 Park Avenue South, New York, NY 10016
        First published in Great Britain by Zambezi Publishing
                    © 2002 by Sasha Fenton
            Distributed in Canada by Sterling Publishing
    ^{c}/o Canadian Manda Group, One Atlantic Avenue, Suite 105
                Toronto, Ontario, Canada M6K 3E7
        Distributed in Australia by Capricorn Link (Australia) Pty. Ltd.
            P.O. Box 704, Windsor, NSW 2756 Australia

            Sterling ISBN 1-4027-0190-X

Sasha Fenton

Sasha's mother was mildly interested in palmistry, and she also had prophetic dreams and "feelings". Perhaps it was her mother's acceptance of psychism that made Sasha more than usually open to these ideas herself. In the event, Sasha took an interest in palmistry and astrology from an early age, and she began to give professional consultations in the early 1970s, adding Tarot to her list of accomplishments at the behest of her clients.

Sasha joined the British Astrological and Psychic Society (BAPS) in 1982 and gained certificates in astrology, palmistry, Tarot and clairvoyance shortly afterwards. She toured the Mind, Body and Spirit festivals with BAPS and started to write for their magazine, Mercury. Her clients urged her to write a book on the Tarot, as there was nothing suitable for a beginner. "Fortune Telling by Tarot Cards" was the result, it has sold over half a million copies, and Sasha has now revised and expanded it, publishing it this time through Zambezi Publishing.

Including six years of the popular annual astroguide series together with her close writing partner, Jonathan Dee, Sasha has now written over 100 further books on all aspects of divination, with total sales in excess of six million copies. Apart from her writing, lecturing, appearances on television and radio shows, Sasha has also acted as Secretary and President of BAPS, has been on the committee of the British Panel on Astrological Education and the Writers' Guild of Great Britain, and had a regular television spot on United Artists for five years.

She now runs Zambezi Publishing in the west of England with her husband, Jan Budkowski. Sasha's first husband, Tony Fenton, died and she married Jan after meeting him at an astrology seminar in Johannesburg. Jan has given up a long career in banking, and moved to England with Sasha. Sasha has two lovely children and grandchildren, with all of whom she has great fun, apart from tripping over their toys...

Dedication
To Judith Stewart and Vivien Watchorn;
Good friends are worth more than treasure...

Contents

Are you Typical of your Sun Sign?

Some people are aware that they are absolutely typical of their Sun sign. Their appearance fits the standard description, while their character, career and relationships follow the prescribed patterns laid down in Sun sign books. Others can see something of themselves in Sun sign descriptions but they also find discrepancies, while yet others feel that they are not at all typical of their Sun sign. Many people have relatives, friends or colleagues who share the same Sun sign as themselves, and they may notice many similarities to themselves, but also a few differences. There are many possible astrological reasons for the diversification within each sign, but this book demonstrates two factors that are easy for a complete beginner in astrology to understand and to use. The odd thing is that, despite the fact that this system is so simple and also so effective, it is not as frequently used by western astrologers as it is in the east.

Decans and Dwaads

A sign of the zodiac can be divided into three sections that are called Decans, and each Decan can be divided into four Dwaads. Thus, you can choose to look at your Sun sign, and any one of three Decans or twelve Dwaads within that sign. (Dwaad is pronounced like "hard").

Sun Sign		
1st. Decan	2nd. Decan	3rd. Decan

1st. Dwaad	2nd. Dwaad	3rd. Dwaad	4th. Dwaad	5th. Dwaad	6th. Dwaad	7th. Dwaad	8th. Dwaad	9th. Dwaad	10th. Dwaad	11th. Dwaad	12th. Dwaad

The division of each Sun sign into twelve Dwaads means that people born even a day or two apart from each other will exhibit variations in their personalities.

This system doesn't rely upon a person being born in a specific year or a particular time of day, which means that someone who was born into a completely different generation from yours, but whose birthday is close to your own, may have more in common with you than someone else who shares your Sun sign, but whose birthday is a week or so away from yours.

It is extremely easy to check out the Decan and Dwaad for your own Sun sign in the Decan and Dwaad calendar given in this book. When you have found them, you can look up the interpretations to discover what they have to say. Once you have checked out the picture for yourself, you can do the same for your loved ones, friends and others.

Predicting the Future

Even a complete beginner will find it easy to progress the Sun sign in order to check out trends and events for any year of your life. All you need to be able to do is to count.

For Astrologers

Those of you who are deeply into astrology and who need absolute accuracy will be glad to know that in the calendar section of this book, I present the Decans and Dwaads in degree form in addition to simply giving the dates for them. This means that you can easily check out the Decans and Dwaads for the Moon, Ascendant, planets, Midheaven or anything else that interests you.

Those who struggle to rectify an Ascendant will find the Decan and Dwaad system of immense help in plotting this. Whether you are a total beginner in astrology, a hobby astrologer or a professional consultant, a working knowledge of Decans and Dwaads can only help to increase your knowledge and understanding.

If you have ever struggled to understand the differences between a pair of twins, you will soon discover how easy it is to check out the Ascendant and Midheaven for Dwaad differences between the two birthcharts. You can also apply the Decan and Dwaad system to any predictive technique such as transits, secondary directions, solar arc directions, solar returns and anything else you care to use. In short, this book has something for everybody - from those who don't know the first thing about astrology, to those who have been working with it for years.

Sun Signs and Decans

Sun Signs

Astrologers use the term Sun signs, you may say star signs or signs of the zodiac or you may ask someone what sign they were born under. The names may differ but they all mean the same thing. The signs of the zodiac are ancient names given to the constellations of stars that lie along the ecliptic, which is the apparent path of the Sun around the earth. Since the advent of telescopes, we know that it is the Earth that orbits the Sun, and that the changing view of stars that appear behind it is similar to the changing view and perspective that you would see in the background if you walked around a tree or some other object.

Those of us who live in areas where the clocks are put forward in spring and back in autumn are accustomed to the fact that this happens at a regular time, e.g. 2 a.m. on a Sunday morning in the British Isles. This man-made arrangement doesn't apply to the movement of the Earth, so the Sun signs don't change from one to another at a set time or even a set day each year. Newspapers and populist astrology books can only print average dates for the start of each sign. This means that for those of you who use the date system that I give in this book, rather than the degree system that astrologers use (which I also give in this book), may have to check out two adjacent signs in order to see which fits you best. If you decide that you would like to know the exact degree of your Sun sign, or indeed of anything else on your birthchart, you can always consult an astrologer or send off to an astrology service for this. If you can give the astrologer a reasonably correct date, time and place of birth, you will be in a position to check out far more than just your Sun sign.

The list below gives the average dates for each Sun sign:

Average Sun Sign Dates

Aries	March 21 to April 19
Taurus	April 20 to May 20
Gemini	May 21 to June 21
Cancer	June 22 to July 22
Leo	July 23 to August 22
Virgo	August 23 to September 22
Libra	September 23 to October 22
Scorpio	October 23 to November 21
Sagittarius	November 22 to December 21
Capricorn	December 22 to January 20
Aquarius	January 21 to February 18
Pisces	February 19 to March 20

The circular chart below shows you how they are arranged in the order that is familiar to astrologers:

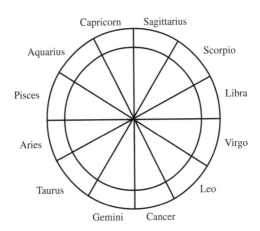

The Decans

Each sign of the zodiac is divided into three Decans, and each of these comprises one third of a sign. The calendar chapter that you will see a little later in this book shows the complete beginner how to find your Sun sign Decan from the date of birth, and it shows the practiced astrologer how to find it by degree. The tables that you will find in this book cover both systems, and both are extremely easy to understand and to use. Once you have worked out which Decan "sub-rules" your sign, look for the relevant chapter for your Sun sign and then the one for your Decan and read both. For example, if you are a Libran with the Sun in the Gemini Decan, read the chapter for Libra first, then the section at the end for the Gemini Decan and finally turn to the chapter on Gemini as a Sun sign for an even fuller interpretation.

The Elements

Each sign of the zodiac belongs to an element of fire, earth, air or water. Each Decan within a sign shares the same element as the original sign. Therefore if you were born under the earth sign of Capricorn, your Sun sign Decan might be Capricorn, Taurus or Virgo, all of which are earth signs. The following list and illustration shows the elemental groups, first in the order that the signs of the zodiac are usually placed, then in their element groups and finally in the familiar astrological circle - which is really three ways of showing the same thing.

The List of Elements

Sign	*Element*
Aries	Fire
Taurus	Earth
Gemini	Air
Cancer	Water
Leo	Fire
Virgo	Earth
Libra	Air
Scorpio	Water
Sagittarius	Fire
Capricorn	Earth
Aquarius	Air
Pisces	Water

Fire Group   - Aries, Leo, Sagittarius
Earth Group   - Taurus, Virgo, Capricorn
Air Group   - Gemini, Libra, Aquarius
Water Group   - Cancer, Scorpio, Pisces

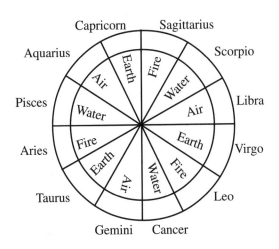

The first sign is Aries, on the left. The other signs rotate anti-clockwise.

The Fire Group
Masculine
Aries, Leo, Sagittarius

Fire sign people do things quickly and they don't allow the grass to grow under their feet. They may commit themselves to a course of action and then regret it because they haven't given themselves enough time to think things through. On the other hand, while others are procrastinating and putting off unpleasant chores or simply not getting their act together, the fire signs are well on the way to finishing the job. Fire people display initiative, courage and leadership qualities. Some are genuinely selfish; while others are so quick to think and act that they leave others behind in their haste to get on with things. Despite their apparent selfishness, many are idealists who really do want to make the world a better place.

Fire sign people have no patience with those who hesitate, and they don't understand that it is not necessarily someone else's karma to grasp every opportunity that comes along. These subjects are quick, intelligent, humorous and generous and they love their friends and family. They become angry when others oppose them and irritable when they are tired or hungry, and they can be extremely cutting when they are wound up, but they rarely sulk. They need a good standard of living to keep up with their spending habits. Fire sign people are often passionate lovers who live life to the full.

Fire sign people are less confident than they appear and they can suddenly lose faith in themselves and become depressed when too much goes wrong. They need a steady and reliable partner who will respect them for their undoubted talents and who doesn't seek to undermine them. In turn, fire sign people need to be reminded to validate their partner and not to build up their own ego at the expense of others.

Fire sign people are often worryingly underweight as children but they soon get over this and they can become quite heavy later in life.

The Earth Group
Feminine
Taurus, Virgo, Capricorn

These are practical, diligent and hard-working people who are happiest when they are doing something useful. They can be relied upon, and even through it might take them a while to get around to things, they usually get there in the end. These people are more ambitious than they appear and they may be shrewd operators in politics or in business. Their drawbacks are sometimes a lack of speed when action is needed, stubbornness and greed and distaste for chancy ventures or of spending money unnecessarily.

Most earth sign people are family types who need the security of a good relationship. They rarely walk away from family responsibility, even when one or two family members are difficult to cope with. These subjects are sensual and loving, especially in a relationship that is comfortable and that gives them confidence. They may have a creative streak, although this manifests itself in different ways for each sign. Shrewd and cautious, they need material and emotional security and they can put up with a lot in order to get it. Many earth types appear tight-fisted, they can be shortsighted about financial matters and this is often due to a real or imagined fear of poverty.

The Air Group
Masculine
Gemini, Libra, Aquarius

The air sign mind is always active. Whether they are humming tunes in their head or playing out ideas and daydreams, their brains are rarely still. Many of them are sociable and friendly and their homes may be filled with neighbors, friends and relatives who pop in or stay for a night or two. Many are good at crafts, handiwork and mechanical tasks and most seem to be able to cope very well with household tasks such as decorating or do-it-themselves jobs. Some love to collect tools, equipment or gadgets. They come up with wonderfully inventive answers to other people's problems, although they often find it hard to solve their own. They are excellent communicators and they may spend hours on the phone or the computer. They can be restless and tenser than they appear and they need a mildly sporting outlet or a change of scene on occasion to help them keep a healthy balance. Many are excellent teachers.

Air sign people are sympathetic to the plight of others, although they aren't good at shouldering the burdens of others for too long as this wears down their own delicate nervous systems. They may seek to protect their sensitive nerves by behaving in an unfeeling manner towards those who are close to them. Most air sign people are hopeless with those who are sick and they may lack patience with family members who become ill or downhearted. Air sign people can lose touch with reality, either by worrying about things that are not important or by living in a kind of fantasy-land.

The Water Group
Feminine
Cancer, Scorpio, Pisces

Water sign people respond slowly when asked a question and they turn round slowly when called. These people need time to grasp new ideas because they need to filter them through their feelings before they can make up their minds. Their feelings run deep and they can be very emotional. When upset, they sulk, brood and they can even be cruel towards those who are close to them. They are extremely intuitive, they sum people up accurately and they tend to feel everything that is going on in the surrounding atmosphere. They use this knowledge to avoid falling into traps that others simply don't see. Water sign people can be attracted to the world of business where their shrewdness and good grasp of money-matters stands them in good stead. Trust is important to them and they prefer to ally themselves to those who they can trust and rely upon.

Water sign people can love very deeply, but some of them save their greatest love for their children or for animals. They keep sensitive feelings hidden, sometimes even from themselves, and this allows irritation and resentment to build up. Once this happens, they either fall into depression or explode - much to the surprise and hurt of those who are around them. Water sign people are restless and they like to get out and about with their work and their social life, they also love to travel and explore new places. Having said this, they also need a base, a secure home and an office, shop or workshop that they can call their own. Environments are important to them and too much noise or disturbance upsets them.

The Genders

Every fire and air sign is called *masculine* and every earth and water sign is called *feminine*. This division has nothing to do with sexuality, but with personality types. Some astrologers call these divisions *positive* or *negative*, which are different names for the same thing, another term might be *extrovert* and *introvert* or even *Yang* and *Yin*.

All fire and air signs are masculine, all earth and water signs are feminine.

The Qualities

Each sign of the zodiac belongs to a *quality*, and these are named *cardinal, fixed* and *mutable*. Each Decan within a sign will have a different quality. For example, Sagittarius is a mutable sign but only the first Decan, which is also Sagittarius, is mutable, the other two are Aries, which is cardinal, and Leo, which is fixed. There are two masculine and two feminine signs from each quality group.

The List of Qualities

Sign	Quality
Aries	Cardinal
Taurus	Fixed
Gemini	Mutable
Cancer	Cardinal
Leo	Fixed
Virgo	Mutable
Libra	Cardinal
Scorpio	Fixed
Sagittarius	Mutable
Capricorn	Cardinal
Aquarius	Fixed
Pisces	Mutable

The Signs Grouped in Qualities

Cardinal - Aries, Cancer, Libra, Capricorn

Fixed - Taurus, Leo, Scorpio, Aquarius

Mutable - Gemini, Virgo, Sagittarius, Pisces

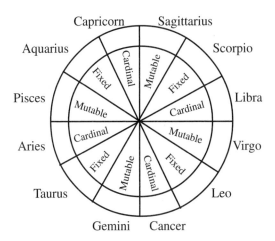

The first sign is Aries, on the left. The other signs rotate anti-clockwise.

The Cardinal Group

Aries, Cancer, Libra, Capricorn

Cardinal types don't let the grass grow under their feet and they are inclined to do what they think is best for themselves, their family or their group. They can put themselves out to fit in with others where necessary, but they can't leave their own needs too far out in the cold.

When the chips are down, they know that they can depend upon themselves. Once they have made up their minds (and this includes the vacillating sign of Libra), they can't be pushed from their path. Cardinal people take advantage of opportunities, they make the most of them and they can be good leaders as long as they allow others an opinion and an opportunity to use their creativity.

One thing they are often good at is motivating and encouraging others, but they may then ask or expect too much of them. Despite the strength of this type, their confidence can evaporate and they need the support of a partner or at the very least a couple of good friends.

The Fixed Group
Taurus, Leo, Scorpio, Aquarius

Fixed sign people try to maintain the status quo, and most prefer a well-ordered life because too much change makes them uncomfortable.

Taureans, Leos and Scorpios need financial security and they fear getting into debt, although Aquarians are less concerned about this. A happy relationship and emotional security is important to these people, and they try to work out the problems within a relationship, if at all possible, rather than giving up at the first hurdle.

All fixed sign people are obstinate, which may make their life and the lives of those around them difficult in some ways, but this obstinacy does bring benefits, in that when these people take on a large task, they do it thoroughly and see it through to a conclusion.

Fixed sign people can put up with boredom and repetition if a job requires it, but outside of work they enjoy change and novelty as much as any other type. They have a responsible attitude to life and they take their duties seriously.

The Mutable Group
Gemini, Virgo, Sagittarius, Pisces

Mutable signs need variety and change, and this may take them into careers that ensure that each day is different from the next. Some prefer the kind of job that takes them from one place to another, while others travel far afield. Many work in one place, but deal with a variety of people or tasks during the course of each day.

Mutable sign people may choose unconventional jobs or life-styles because it is more important for their work to fit in with their beliefs or to fulfil their spiritual needs. Many work in fields that either expand people's minds, such as writing or publishing, while others work in fields that expand their experiences, such as the travel trade or psychic work. These people sometimes choose to work in jobs that improve the lot of others, even though they can't earn much or climb the ladder of material success this way.

There is a streak of independence and unconventionality about all the mutable signs, although this is less obvious in Gemini and Virgo, than it is in Sagittarius and Pisces.

Many mutable sign types marry when young and start their families early. However, these early relationships all too frequently break up and they may go through a period of experimentation with a variety of partners before settling down again.

Putting it All Together

The following table shows the attributes for each sign. The first Decan in any sign is always a duplicate or repeat of that sign, so that, for example, the Decans for Aries are Aries, Leo, Sagittarius.

1st. Decan (as Sunsign)	Second Decan	Third Decan
Aries/Fire/Cardinal	Leo/Fire/Fixed	Sagittarius/Fire/Mutable
Taurus/Earth/Fixed	Virgo/Earth/Mutable	Capricorn/Earth/Cardinal
Gemini/Air/Mutable	Libra/Air/Cardinal	Aquarius/Air/Fixed
Cancer/Water/Cardinal	Scorpio/Water/Fixed	Pisces/Water/Mutable
Leo/Fire/Fixed	Sagittarius/Fire/Mutable	Aries/Fire/Cardinal
Virgo/Earth/Mutable	Capricorn/Earth/Cardinal	Taurus/Earth/Fixed
Libra/Air/Cardinal	Aquarius/Air/Fixed	Gemini/Air/Mutable
Scorpio/Water/Fixed	Pisces/Water/Mutable	Cancer/Water/Cardinal
Sagittarius/Fire/Mutable	Aries/Fire/Cardinal	Leo/Fire/Fixed
Capricorn/Earth/Cardinal	Taurus/Earth/Fixed	Virgo/Earth/Mutable
Aquarius/Air/Fixed	Gemini/Air/Mutable	Libra/Air/Cardinal
Pisces/Water/Mutable	Cancer/Water/Cardinal	Scorpio/Water/Fixed

Some Technical Information

The information below may appear complex to a beginner, but relax - it isn't essential, but it will interest students of astrology.
* Some astrologers call Decans by the name Decanates. Either is acceptable, but I have stuck to Decans in this book.
* The word Decan comes from the Latin for ten and it refers to the fact that a Decan contains ten of the 30 degrees in each sign.
* Each sign contains 30 degrees and each degree contains 60 minutes.
* Each sign starts at 0 degrees 0 minutes and ends at 29 degrees 59 minutes.

The following example shows you the picture for one sign of the zodiac, using the degree system.

Cancer		
1st. Decan: *Cancer*	**2nd. Decan:** *Scorpio*	**3rd. Decan:** *Pisces*
0 deg. 0 min. to: 9 deg. 59 min.	10 deg. 0 min. to: 19 deg. 59 min.	20 deg. 0 min. to: 29 deg. 59 min.

Example: If we look at George W. Bush, we see that he was born on the 6th of July, 1946 and his Sun position is 13 degrees 47 minutes of Cancer, so his Cancerian Sun sign is subruled by the Scorpio Decan. If President Bush were reading my book, I would suggest that he read the chapters for Cancer plus the Scorpio Decan, and then Scorpio.

The Planets

Every zodiac sign is associated with a planet, and astrologers use their knowledge of the planets in association with the Decans. The planets Uranus, Neptune and Pluto, and the planetoid Chiron, were only discovered within the last three centuries.

Sign	Planet
Aries	Mars
Taurus	Venus
Gemini	Mercury
Cancer	The Moon
Leo	The Sun
Virgo	Mercury (some astrologers also use Chiron)
Libra	Venus
Scorpio	Pluto (and in olden times, Mars)
Sagittarius	Jupiter
Capricorn	Saturn
Aquarius	Uranus (and in olden times, Saturn)
Pisces	Neptune (and in olden times, Jupiter)

Those who understand the energies of the planets will soon see how they influence the Decans. For instance Mercury adds quickness, humor, healing talent and a touch of magic when the Gemini Decan is in operation.

Summing Up

* There are three *Decans* in each sign of the zodiac.

* All three Decans share the same gender and element as the original sign. The first Decan is a repeat of the original sign; the other two are different.

* Each Decan comprises ten degrees of a sign, which is also approximately ten days of a year. (Remember a circle comprises 360 degrees, while a year contains 365 or 366 days.)

* Each Decan has a different *quality* from the others in the same sign; the first repeats the sign, so it shares its quality, and the other two are always different.

* Keep an eye on the *planet* that is associated with the Decan. For example, the second Decan of Capricorn is Taurus, so the planet that rules the Decan is Venus.

* If you are deeply interested in astrology, look around the chart to see how the planets that rule the Sun and Decan are faring. For example, if you are looking at someone whose ascendant is in Virgo, see what sign, Decan (and Dwaad) Mercury occupies natally, by progression, and even what is happening to transiting Mercury at any one time.

And Finally...

You will find interpretations for every Sun sign and its Decans in this book.

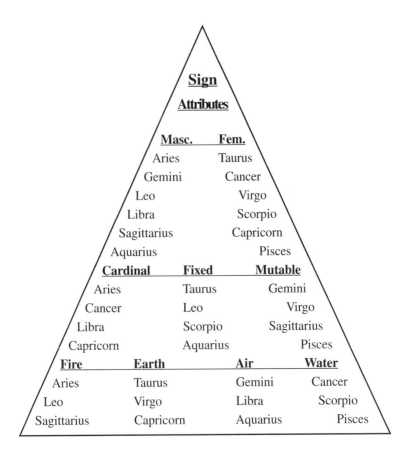

A visual summary of Sun Sign Attributes

Dwaads

The word Dwaad (pronounced like hard) comes from Indian astrology, and it is one of the many mathematical divisions that are now more commonly used in Asian and Vedic astrology than by westerners, and it is one of the few that is easy to plot and to understand. You will discover how to look up your Dwaad in the calendar chapters that follow this one.

For Beginners

Just as the Decans divide each sign of the zodiac into three segments, the Dwaads divide each sign into twelve segments. The first Dwaad is a repeat of the original sign, with the other eleven following on in sequence. If we take the sign of Scorpio as an example, the first Dwaad is Scorpio; the second is Sagittarius and so on through all twelve signs, ending with Libra. If you look at the circular chart that follows, you will see the pattern. You can trace the Dwaads yourself, by picking out your own Sign and then working round the wheel in an anti-clockwise direction until you end up at the sign that precedes your own.

Once you get used to the system, you will discover that each Decan starts with a Dwaad of the same sign. If you look at the following example for the sign of Taurus, you will soon see what I mean. When you become accustomed to using the system, you will find it easy to work out the Decans and Dwaads in your head.

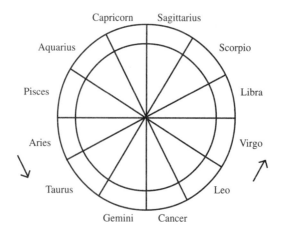

Working out your Dwaads...

Example: Sun Sign - Taurus
First Decan: Taurus (Dwaads: Taurus, Gemini, Cancer, Leo)
Second Decan: Virgo (Dwaads: Virgo, Libra, Scorpio, Sagittarius)
Third Decan: Capricorn (Dwaads: Capricorn, Aquarius, Pisces, Aries)

Read the instructions for using the calendar tables and you will soon see which is your Sun sign Dwaad. It is easy. If you have any doubt about which of two Dwaads you come under, read both. If you are an astrologer but you don't have an accurate birth time to work from, or if you need to double check, you can refer to the table that uses dates rather than degrees for help. If all else fails, find the two Dwaads that are closest and read both.

Genders, Elements, Qualities and Planets
Only the first Dwaad will be a repeat of the sign with its original gender, element and quality, but the other eleven could have any combination because the whole zodiac is used. Thus a person born under one Sun sign may be sub-ruled by a Dwaad that has a different gender, element and quality and which is ruled by a totally different type of planet.

A person born right at the start of a sign where the Decan and Dwaad are the same as the sign itself should be pretty typical of his sign. However, even then the position of nearby planets, the ascendant, the Moon and other features on a chart will still exert a variety of different influences.

Some Notes for Astrologers

Twins may or may not have their Sun in different Dwaads but there is a very strong chance that their Moon, Ascendant or Midheaven will differ.

A person's Sun sign, Rising sign or Moon sign can easily turn up in a relative's chart as a Decan or Dwaad sign. In my case, my Sun sign is Leo sub-ruled by the Aries Decan, and the Taurus Dwaad, while my father's Sun sign was Aries in the Leo Decan and his Moon was in Taurus. I can't tell you about my mother's chart, as I don't have an accurate date of birth for her.

If you are not absolutely certain of the correct position of an Ascendant, checking out the Decans and Dwaads can help. You can double check by looking at the Midheaven to see if the sign, Decan and Dwaad match the person's aims, objectives, goals, ambitions and career choices.

Using the Decan and Dwaad Calendar

This calendar is a two-tier system that I have designed for use either by total beginners or by astrologers. You will find two calendars for each sign (see the example shown below); the first gives you the picture by date and the second by degree. If you are a beginner, use the calendar for your sign that goes by date rather than by degree.

Beginners Method
* Choose the calendar that goes by date.
* Look at the bottom row and select your day of birth. For example, 3/31 means March 31st.
* Look at the next row up, to see which Dwaad you come under.
* Look above again to see which Decan you come under.
* The top row simply shows the Sun sign covered by the dates in the table.

Aries by Date											
1st. Decan Aries				2nd. Decan Leo				3rd. Decan Sagit.			
ARIES	TAURUS	GEMINI	CANCER	LEO	VIRGO	LIBRA	SCORPIO	SAGIT.	CAPRIC.	AQUARIUS	PISCES
3/21	3/23	3/25	3/28	3/31	4/2	4/5	4/7	4/10	4/12	4/15	4/17

The Degree Calendar

The second calendar for each sign is suitable for those of you who have a natal chart to hand, and who know how to read it. This shows the picture for your sign by degree and it works in exactly the same way as the date calendar.

Aries by Degree										
1st. Decan Aries				2nd. Decan Leo				3rd. Decan Sagit.		
ARIES	TAURUS	GEMINI	CANCER	LEO	VIRGO	LIBRA	SCORPIO	SAGIT.	CAPRIC.	AQUARIUS	PISCES
0	2.30	5	7.30	10	12.30	15	17.30	20	22.30	25	27.30

Astrologers Method

* Check your degree in the bottom line.

* Look up to the next line to see which Dwaad you come under.

* Remember to use the degrees and minutes, because if your exact Sun sign figure is something like 12 deg. 24 mins. you will come under one Dwaad, while if it is 12 deg. 35 mins. you will come under the next.

* Look up again to see which Decan you come under.

* The top row shows the Sun sign.

The Decan and Dwaad Calendar

If you dive into the Decan and Dwaad calendar without knowing how to read it, remember that old saying, "When in doubt, read the instructions", so go back now and read through the instructions given in the previous chapter!

Once you have found the Decan and Dwaad for your Sun sign, make a note of them, then find the chapter on your Sun sign and read through that, plus the relevant Decan and Dwaad information that you will find at the end of the chapter. If you want to know more about the signs that your Decan and Dwaad occupy, treat them as Sun signs and read the relevant chapters. For example, if you turn up a Leo Dwaad, read the chapter for Leo as a Sun sign. You can get even more information if you look up the gender, element and quality of the Decan or Dwaad that you wish to investigate, in the chapter covering those items.

If you know the exact position of your Ascendant, you will find its attributes covered in this book as well. For any planet or any other feature that you wish to look at, read through the chapter on the gender, element and quality of whatever Decan or Dwaad sign you are investigating, and also read through the Sun sign chapter that relates to the zodiac sign in question. For instance, for a planet in a Virgo Dwaad, read the Virgo Sun sign section.

~~ ARIES ~~

Aries by Date

1st. Decan Aries				2nd. Decan Leo				3rd. Decan Sagittarius			
Aries	Taurus	Gemini	Cancer	Leo	Virgo	Libra	Scorpio	Sagit.	Capric.	Aquarius	Pisces
3/21	3/23	3/25	3/28	3/31	4/2	4/5	4/7	4/10	4/12	4/15	4/17

Aries by Degree

1st. Decan Aries				2nd. Decan Leo				3rd. Decan Sagittarius			
Aries	Taurus	Gemini	Cancer	Leo	Virgo	Libra	Scorpio	Sagit.	Capric.	Aquarius	Pisces
0	2.30	5	7.30	10	12.30	15	17.30	20	22.30	25	27.30

~~ TAURUS ~~

Taurus by Date

1st. Decan Taurus				2nd. Decan Virgo				3rd. Decan Capricorn			
Taurus	Gemini	Cancer	Leo	Virgo	Libra	Scorpio	Sagit	Capric	Aquarius	Pisces	Aries
4/20	4/22	4/25	4/27	4/30	5/2	5/5	5/7	5/10	5/13	5/15	5/18

Taurus by Degree

1st. Decan Taurus				2nd. Decan Virgo				3rd. Decan Capricorn			
Taurus	Gemini	Cancer	Leo	Virgo	Libra	Scorpio	Sagit	Capric	Aquarius	Pisces	Aries
0	2.30	5	7.30	10	12.30	15	17.30	20	22.30	25	27.30

~~ GEMINI ~~

Gemini by Date

1st. Decan Gemini				2nd. Decan Libra				3rd. Decan Aquarius			
Gemini	Cancer	Leo	Virgo	Libra	Scorpio	Sagit.	Capric.	Aquarius	Pisces.	Aries	Taurus
5/21	5/23	5/26	5/28	5/31	6/2	6/5	6/8	6/11	6/13	6/16	6/18

Gemini by Degree

1st. Decan Gemini				2nd. Decan Libra				3rd. Decan Aquarius			
Gemini	Cancer	Leo	Virgo	Libra	Scorpio	Sagit.	Capric.	Aquarius	Pisces.	Aries	Taurus
0	2.30	5	7.30	10	12.30	15	17.30	20	22.30	25	27.30

~~ CANCER ~~

Cancer by Date

1st. Decan Cancer				2nd. Decan Scorpio				3rd. Decan Pisces			
Cancer	Leo	Virgo	Libra	Scorpio	Sagit.	Capric.	Aquarius	Pisces	Aries	Taurus	Gemini
6/21	6/24	6/26	6/29	7/2	7/4	7/7	7/9	7/12	7/15	7/17	7/20

Cancer by Degree

1st. Decan Cancer				2nd. Decan Scorpio				3rd. Decan Pisces			
Cancer	Leo	Virgo	Libra	Scorpio	Sagit.	Capric.	Aquarius	Pisces	Aries	Taurus	Gemini
0	2.30	5	7.30	10	12.30	15	17.30	20	22.30	25	27.30

~~ LEO ~~

Leo by Date

1st. Decan Leo				2nd. Decan Sagittarius				3rd. Decan Aries			
Leo	Virgo	Libra	Scorpio	Sagit.	Capric.	Aquarius	Pisces	Aries	Taurus	Gemini	Cancer
7/23	7/25	7/27	7/30	8/2	8/4	8/7	8/9	8/12	8/15	8/17	8/20

Leo by Degree

1st. Decan Leo				2nd. Decan Sagittarius				3rd. Decan Aries			
Leo	Virgo	Libra	Scorpio	Sagit.	Capric.	Aquarius	Pisces	Aries	Taurus	Gemini	Cancer
0	2.30	5	7.30	10	12.30	15	17.30	20	22.30	25	27.30

~~ VIRGO ~~

Virgo by Date

1st. Decan Virgo				2nd. Decan Capricorn				3rd. Decan Taurus			
Virgo	Libra	Scorpio	Sagit.	Capric.	Aquarius	Pisces	Aries	Taurus	Gemini	Cancer	Leo
8/23	8/25	8/28	8/30	9/2	9/4	9/7	9/9	9/12	9/15	9/17	9/20

Virgo by Degree

1st. Decan Virgo				2nd. Decan Capricorn				3rd. Decan Taurus			
Virgo	Libra	Scorpio	Sagit.	Capric.	Aquarius	Pisces	Aries	Taurus	Gemini	Cancer	Leo
0	2.30	5	7.30	10	12.30	15	17.30	20	22.30	25	27.30

~~ LIBRA ~~

Libra by Date

1st. Decan Libra				2nd. Decan Aquarius				3rd. Decan Gemini			
Libra	Scorpio	Sagit.	Capric.	Aquarius	Pisces	Aries	Taurus	Gemini	Cancer	Leo	Virgo
9/23	9/25	9/28	9/30	10/3	10/5	10/8	10/10	10/13	10/15	10/18	10/20

Libra by Degree

1st. Decan Libra				2nd. Decan Aquarius				3rd. Decan Gemini			
Libra	Scorpio	Sagit.	Capric.	Aquarius	Pisces	Aries	Taurus	Gemini	Cancer	Leo	Virgo
0	2.30	5	7.30	10	12.30	15	17.30	20	22.30	25	27.30

~~ SCORPIO ~~

Scorpio by Date

1st. Decan Scorpio				2nd. Decan Pisces				3rd. Decan Cancer			
Scorpio	Sagit.	Capric.	Aquarius	Pisces	Aries	Taurus	Gemini	Cancer	Leo	Virgo	Libra
10/23	10/25	10/28	10/30	11/2	11/4	11/7	11/9	11/12	11/14	11/17	11/19

Scorpio by Degree

1st. Decan Scorpio				2nd. Decan Pisces				3rd. Decan Cancer			
Scorpio	Sagit.	Capric.	Aquarius	Pisces	Aries	Taurus	Gemini	Cancer	Leo	Virgo	Libra
0	2.30	5	7.30	10	12.30	15	17.30	20	22.30	25	27.30

~~ SAGITTARIUS ~~

Sagittarius by Date

1st. Decan Sagittarius				2nd. Decan Aries				3rd. Decan Leo			
Sagit.	Capric.	Aquarius	Pisces	Aries	Taurus	Gemini	Cancer	Leo	Virgo	Libra	Scorpio
11/22	11/24	11/27	11/29	12/2	12/4	12/7	12/9	12/12	12/14	12/16	12/19

Sagittarius by Degree

1st. Decan Sagittarius				2nd. Decan Aries				3rd. Decan Leo			
Sagit.	Capric.	Aquarius	Pisces	Aries	Taurus	Gemini	Cancer	Leo	Virgo	Libra	Scorpio
0	2.30	5	7.30	10	12.30	15	17.30	20	22.30	25	27.30

~~ CAPRICORN ~~

Capricorn by Date

1st. Decan Capricorn				2nd. Decan Taurus				3rd. Decan Virgo			
Capric.	Aquarius	Pisces	Aries	Taurus	Gemini	Cancer	Leo	Virgo	Libra	Scorpio	Sagit.
12/22	12/24	12/27	12/29	1/1	1/3	1/6	1/8	1/11	1/13	1/16	1/18

Capricorn by Degree

1st. Decan Capricorn				2nd. Decan Taurus				3rd. Decan Virgo			
Capric.	Aquarius	Pisces	Aries	Taurus	Gemini	Cancer	Leo	Virgo	Libra	Scorpio	Sagit.
0	2.30	5	7.30	10	12.30	15	17.30	20	22.30	25	27.30

~~ AQUARIUS ~~

Aquarius by Date

1st. Decan Aquarius				2nd. Decan Gemini				3rd. Decan Libra			
Aquarius	Pisces	Aries	Taurus	Gemini	Cancer	Leo	Virgo	Libra	Scorpio	Sagit.	Capric.
1/21	1/23	1/26	1/28	1/31	2/2	2/4	2/6	2/9	2/11	2/14	2/16

Aquarius by Degree

1st. Decan Aquarius				2nd. Decan Gemini				3rd. Decan Libra			
Aquarius	Pisces	Aries	Taurus	Gemini	Cancer	Leo	Virgo	Libra	Scorpio	Sagit.	Capric.
0	2.30	5	7.30	10	12.30	15	17.30	20	22.30	25	27.30

~~ PISCES ~~

Pisces by Date

1st. Decan Pisces				2nd. Decan Cancer				3rd. Decan Scorpio			
Pisces	Aries	Taurus	Gemini	Cancer	Leo	Virgo	Libra	Scorpio	Sagit.	Capric.	Aquarius
2/19	2/22	2/24	2/27	3/1	3/3	3/6	3/8	3/11	3/13	3/16	3/18

Pisces by Degree

1st. Decan Pisces				2nd. Decan Cancer				3rd. Decan Scorpio			
Pisces	Aries	Taurus	Gemini	Cancer	Leo	Virgo	Libra	Scorpio	Sagit.	Capric.	Aquarius
0	2.30	5	7.30	10	12.30	15	17.30	20	22.30	25	27.30

Sun Sign Aries

March 21 to April 19
Ruling planet: Mars
Symbol: The Ram
Gender: Masculine
This indicates an extrovert, active, courageous and somewhat pushy nature.

The Element of Fire

Aries, Leo, Sagittarius

Fire sign people do things quickly and they don't allow the grass to grow under their feet. They may commit themselves to a course of action and then regret it because they haven't given themselves enough time to think things through. On the other hand, while others are procrastinating and putting off unpleasant chores or simply not getting their act together, the fire signs are well on the way to finishing the job. Fire people display initiative, courage and leadership qualities. Some are genuinely selfish; while others are so quick to think and act that they leave others behind in their haste to get on with things. Despite their apparent selfishness, many are idealists who really do want to make the world a better place.

Fire sign people have no patience with those who hesitate, and they don't understand that it is not necessarily someone else's karma to grasp every opportunity that comes along. These subjects are quick, intelligent, humorous and generous and they love their friends and family. They become angry when others oppose them and irritable when they are tired or hungry, and they can be extremely cutting when they are wound up, but they rarely sulk. They need a good standard of living to keep up with their spending habits. Fire sign people are often passionate lovers who live life to the full.

Fire sign people are less confident than they appear and they can suddenly lose faith in themselves and become depressed when too much goes wrong. They need a steady and reliable partner who will respect them for their undoubted talents and who doesn't seek to undermine them. In turn, fire sign people need to be reminded to validate their partner and not to build up their own ego at the expense of others.

Fire sign people are often worryingly underweight as children but they soon get over this and they can become quite heavy later in life.

The Cardinal Quality
Aries, Cancer, Libra, Capricorn
Cardinal types don't let the grass grow under their feet and they are inclined to do what they think is best for themselves, their family or their group. They can put themselves out to fit in with others where necessary, but they can't leave their own needs too far out in the cold. When the chips are down but they know that they can depend upon themselves. Once they have made their minds up (and this includes the vacillating sign of Libra), they can't be pushed from their path. Cardinal people take advantage of opportunities, they make the most of them and they can be good leaders as long as they allow others an opinion and an opportunity to use their creativity. One thing they are often good at is motivating and encouraging others, but they may then ask or expect too much of others. Despite the strength of this type, their confidence can evaporate and they need the support of a partner or at the very least a couple of good friends.

Aries Looks

Most Arians are average height or on the short side but body shapes can vary between chunky, rounded and inclined to gain weight or quite slim with fibrous muscles. The slim type may be sporty and energetic and he often chooses a career that exercises his strength and muscles and keeps him from putting on weight. The chunky type is more likely to be sedentary or desk bound. Most Arians have a prominent backside. The rounded type has small features with flat cheekbones, and in white races, usually fair or reddish hair. The hard-bodied type has regular features with well-defined eyebrows and thick dark hair that grows fairly low on the forehead. Aries men often lose their hair quite early in life, but they do say that bald men are sexy!

Main Characteristics

Arians have a take-charge attitude and they like to be in the center of activity. They are happiest when they are in the lead or at the head of an organization. They work hard and play hard and many have enough energy left over to lead pretty hectic sex lives. Many have an idealistic outlook that leads them to become involved in some form of politics. Most are impetuous, enthusiastic, idealistic, sometimes argumentative, softhearted and kind and occasionally amazingly shortsighted.

General Character

The average Arian is intelligent, quick, friendly, outgoing and talkative. He may be a witty raconteur or a real comedian. Some Arians can be sarcastic and critical but even when being bitchy - and despite all their verbal ability, Arians don't usually have loud or penetrating voices. Most Arians read widely and they have a good command of language, grammar and spelling. Some are musical or artistic, especially if they have planets in the nearby signs of Pisces and Taurus and many enjoy singing, dancing or sport.

There is a deeper side to the Arian nature, which often leads these subjects into committees, causes and politics. Part of the motivation for this is the desire to be a leader or to be in the limelight, but Arians are also extremely idealistic. Sometimes when the Arian obtains the position that he craves, it goes to his head and he drops the idealism in favor of throwing his weight around.

The masculine Martial energy makes typical Arians competitive, and this is sometimes openly expressed in sports where the Arian's determination to win at all costs takes him to the top. Other Arians put their energies into their working lives. Even when an Arian doesn't appear on the face of things to be particularly competitive, this streak is bound to be present. Sometimes this competitiveness stems from a fear that others wish to usurp his position or to leave him behind. A typical Arian will always search for a position of prominence, eminence, power or influence. Some Arians are openly aggressive while others are co-operative, but most enjoy a challenge. Most are lovable, humorous, kind and quick to sympathize with those who are in trouble. A few are so self-absorbed that they are impossible to live with, but this type is rare, although there is often a streak of self-preservation that makes it difficult for Ariens to bend over backwards for others to any great extent.

Arians tend to have strong opinions and they may pigeonhole people in unpleasant ways. Some Arians can't stand people of a different color, race, religion or sexual nature. However, the polar opposite is often the case with the Arians actively enjoying the company of people of many different backgrounds, types and walks of life. Another Arian fault is self-indulgence, which may be expressed in overeating, alcoholism or shopping.

Arian Careers

Arians can be found in large organizations that benefit the public. Teaching comes naturally to them, as does work in the armed forces, the police, hospitals or other large organizations. Many are drawn to engineering, draftsmanship, architecture and motor mechanics. They can handle tough jobs or those that require physical strength, often despite not being particularly tall or tough looking. However, one arena that is extremely attractive to this sign is politics and many top politicians in any political party are to be found under this sign. At one point in time, around 40 per cent of British Members of Parliament were Arians. If not attracted to party politics, the Arian might opt for Trade Union leadership, committees, fund-raising groups and so on. They even find their way onto the committees of spiritualist groups.

Arians are happy in supervisory positions and some can cope with self-employment, as long as this involves dealing with people and getting out and about. There are plenty of Arians in the building and allied trades, also engineering, civil engineering, architecture and other technical trades. Oddly enough, many Arians are excellent psychics and many have a religious, philosophical or spiritual side to their natures. If the Arian can't express himself in his job, he will do so in his hobbies. These subjects usually have some kind of hobby or interest beside work and family life. Even when Arians retire, they will find something to do, and this is usually something that helps others.

Aries and Money

Some Arians are generous while others are tight-fisted. Most Arians manage to earn the money that they want and they will take on extra work if necessary to top up their income. They are not great savers, but most will pay off a mortgage at some point and many ensure that they have a pension to fall back on. Some Arians spend fortunes on the things that interest them. Clothes come high on this list, but vehicles, gadgets, sports or hobby equipment and travel may also attract them.

Home is Where the Junk is

Arians love having plenty of everything, so their homes are full of books, gadgets, tools, along with screws, nails, bits of wood and paint that might come in handy some day. Some take on major do-it-yourself jobs and not all have the skill or knowledge to do them properly, and they may leave them half done once the initial enthusiasm wears off. Some are incredibly untidy, but many are neat, clean and house-proud. Most Arians prefer to go out and enjoy life than to sit around in the home and many work hard outside the home and have plenty of other interests to keep them going when not at work. Some love to spend time gardening, doing craftwork, sewing, cooking or acting as secretary for a charity or organization. Many prefer listening to music or a radio program than sitting around and watching the television.

Arian Relationships

These subjects are relaters but they may find it difficult to stay in a marriage. Some go through several relationships, while others try one or two and end up alone. Sometimes this is due to a need for sexual variety and experimentation; sometimes it is simply that the Aries finds it hard to cope with the give and take of marriage. Others are extremely long-suffering and stay in difficult relationships for many years. In some circumstances, the relationship that means the most to them is the one that they have with their children. Arians of both sexes will make considerable sacrifices for their offspring and they try to help them long after they reach adulthood. Aries parents may be domineering, and this can lead to alienation while their children are growing up, but if they learn to cool their tendency to dictate or to lay down rules and regulations, better relations can often be re-established later on.

Most Arian homes are filled with family members, obscure relatives, friends and neighbors. These people love entertaining and having others around, but sometimes they want to be alone for a while.

Sex is another polar matter, because like the Ram, which is their symbol, many Arians are extremely highly sexed. There are some who sublimate their sexual urges into work or politics. The highly sexed variety can also be extremely experimental or even kinky.

Health

On the whole this is a vigorously healthy sign with the only real problem being headaches. Eyes can be a problem, as can sudden infections. If an Arian falls ill, his life may be in danger until the matter is put right. Problems such as strokes, coronary artery disease and sudden incurable forms of cancer are possibilities, but for the most part this is a remarkably healthy and long-lived sign.

A Few stray Facts

Unless the subject belongs to a black or brown race, he can't take too much Sun. Their fair skin means that they burn badly.

No Arian can travel light. I remember one Arian who booked a very nice hotel for his holidays, but also took his tent and groundsheet along with him. Some enjoy sporting holidays, others enjoy seeing interesting places but very few are interested in lying around on a beach.

If you visit an Arian man, he will ensure that you are sitting comfortably, that you have a cup of tea and piece of cake and even something interesting to read. Once you are nicely settled and looking forward to a good old gossip, your Aries host will walk out of the room and leave you. If you want his full concentration, have sex with him!

Arians are clever, knowledgeable and often academic but there is an element of silliness about them that can land them in trouble. In some cases they lack a sense of reality, while in others they can't see the wood for the trees. They can lack common sense.

Aries children are extremely lively and they are often underweight, but most make this up in later life. It is hard for Arians to diet, although some enjoy exercise throughout life and that helps.

Aries women like making cakes.

Aries Decans

The first Decan is also Aries, but the second is Leo and the third is Sagittarius. Read through the brief descriptions below and then turn to the chapters on Leo and Sagittarius for more.

1st Decan, Aries

Pure Aries. Nothing much fazes these people, and those who seek to put them down or stand in their way are in for a shock. Confidence can suddenly evaporate, and the Arian can punish himself when he feels that he has done something silly, and this is when he needs to turn to sympathetic friends for reassurance. Arians need some active hobby or to be involved in a macho job in order to use up excess energy. They aren't short of intelligence but they may lack common sense.

2nd Decan, Leo

The Leo influence makes the Aries more businesslike and also less apt to get carried away by his own success or to fall for his own propaganda. It adds creativity, generosity and a fondness for children and family life, also a love of luxury and good living. The Leo Decan adds tenacity and obstinacy and makes it easier for the Aries to finish what he starts.

3rd Decan, Sagittarius

The Sagittarian influence gives the Arian strong religious or philosophical beliefs and it can lead to great idealism on the one hand, racism or political craziness on the other. Many of these Arians make excellent teachers or lawyers. This placement can also add a great sense of humor. These people need personal freedom and they love to travel or to be involved with foreigners or foreign places.

Aries Dwaads

The first Dwaad is Aries, so no change here. For all other Dwaads, read the chapter on the sign in question and also the brief description given below to see what adjustments or additions are made to the original sign.

Sign	**What is added**
Aries	Pure Aries.
Taurus	Obstinacy, thoroughness, sociability, love of beauty and luxury.
Gemini	Quickness of mind, nervousness, communication ability and dexterity.
Cancer	Love of home and family, business acumen, caution.
Leo	Love of grandeur, leadership qualities, generosity, creativity.
Virgo	Attention to detail, interest in health or research.
Libra	Love of beauty, laziness, sociability, artistic or musical talent.
Scorpio	Thoroughness, tenacity, resentment, skill and dexterity.
Sagittarius	Love of freedom and travel, teaching ability, spirituality, humor.
Capricorn	Ambition, ability to work in a large organization, touchiness.
Aquarius	Originality, eccentricity, fondness for causes, obstinacy.
Pisces	Artistry, lack of common sense, intuition, interest in mysticism.

Sun Sign Taurus

April 20 to May 20
Ruling planet: Venus
Symbol: The Bull
Gender: Feminine

Feminine sign types are introverts who are more thorough and patient than the masculine sign types. These types can put up with quite a lot of hardship.

The Element of Earth

Taurus, Virgo, Capricorn

These are practical, diligent and hard-working people who are happiest when they are doing something useful. They can be relied upon, and even though it might take them a while to get around to things but they usually get there in the end. These people are more ambitious than they appear and they may be shrewd operators in politics or in business. Their drawbacks are sometimes a lack of speed when action is needed, stubbornness, greed and distaste for chancy ventures or of spending money unnecessarily.

Most earth sign people are family types who need the security of a good relationship. They rarely walk away from family responsibility, even when one or two family members are difficult to cope with. These subjects are sensual and loving, especially in a relationship that is comfortable and that gives them confidence. They may have a creative streak, although this manifests itself in different ways for each sign. Shrewd and cautious, they need material and emotional security and they can put up with a lot in order to get it. Many earth types appear tight-fisted, they can be shortsighted about financial matters and this is often due to a real or imagined fear of poverty.

The Fixed Quality
Taurus, Leo, Scorpio, Aquarius

Fixed people try to main the status quo and most prefer a well-ordered life, because too much change makes them uncomfortable. Taureans, Leos and Scorpios need financial security and they fear getting into debt, but Aquarians are less concerned about this. A happy relationship and emotional security is important to these people, and they try to work out the problems within a relationship, if at all possible, rather than giving up at the first hurdle. All fixed sign people are obstinate, which may make their life and the lives of those around them difficult in some ways, but their determination comes to their aid when they take on a large task, because they do it thoroughly and see it through to a conclusion. Fixed sign people can put up with boredom and repetition if a job requires it, but outside of work they enjoy change and novelty as much as any other type. They have a responsible attitude to life and they take their duties seriously.

Taurean Looks

The Taurean body shape is either quite heavily overweight or really slim and there rarely seems to be a middle ground, but even the thin type can put on weight if their lifestyle changes from active to sedentary. The larger Taurean has a large tummy and heavy thighs but it is rare for any Taurean to have a large or prominent backside. Neither type is tall. The eyes are large and attractive, the hair is thick and often with a low hairline. For some reason many Taurean men grow beards and many females pile on cosmetics - it is almost as though they feel a need to hide their faces behind something.

Main Characteristics

Taureans are real family people who love nothing better than to be at home doing things with or for their families. They are steady, reliable and conscientious, but they don't like to be rushed or pushed around. They are renowned for their obstinacy and also their complacency but when roused they can move mountains. Taureans have a highly developed sense of taste and a love of beauty in all its forms.

General Character

Taureans are conventional, preferring a stable home life, a normal job, hobbies and interests that are within normal limits. If they are comfortable with religion, they will attend religious services on a fairly regular basis and some can become deeply involved in a spiritual or even a cult interest. Taureans succeed in their careers due to staying put and get on with the job and some have real executive ability. These people are extremely shrewd, and some are excellent business people, but most seem to prefer a safe and predictable middle-ranking position where their responsible attitude and thoroughness is appreciated. Taureans are intelligent and well read, and they often have a great deal of knowledge about their chosen subject, but they are unlikely to become academics. They often belie their intelligence and knowledge because they don't display it or put on airs and graces.

Taureans are typical middle-class people who work to pay off a mortgage, put their children through school, enjoy meals out with friends and holidays or going to shows and musical events. Some of these subjects are extremely artistic and they will use this artistry in a career or a hobby. They have "safe" hands, which means that they use tools with confidence, make things with their hands and hardly every drop anything. They are dexterous and careful. Taureans hate being rushed, preferring to give themselves time to get everything done in good time. They are usually extremely sociable and they love to go out and to chat and gossip with friends.

Some Taureans are so obsessed with a particular hobbyhorse that they turn every conversation around to it and bore everyone to death, but most are pretty average in their attitude to the things that interest them. Taurean faults can include gluttony, stinginess, laziness and a lack of interest in others. However, most are humorous, sociable, good to their families, quiet and kind.

Taurean Careers

Taurean careers usually include making something or doing something creative and also dealing with the public. This is the sign of the construction engineer, house-builder, woodworker, hairdresser, cake maker, dress designer, make-up artist, gardener or in any other practical field. Most are animal lovers and some choose to work in this field, while on a larger scale, farming and animal husbandry are common Taurean jobs. Another Taurean interest is finance. These people are both shrewd and careful with regard to money-matters and they often find work in careers like banking, where they take care of people's money, and some can make money from investments. Some work as bookkeepers or accountants.

Many Taureans have great speaking voices, and many are also talented singers. They can be drawn to acting and dancing as well as singing. Consider the talent of Taurean singer and dancer, Cher, or in a previous generation, Fred Astaire. They are not usually sporty or into gymnastics because it is the rhythm and music that attracts them. One odd thing is that many Taureans seem to go into Gemini-type careers such as telephone work, working in call centers or organizing teams of workers to go out and fix things but they will express their creative or musical talent in their hobbies. Taureans make reliable employees but they don't live to work. These people view their career as part of their lives rather than the main issue.

Oddly enough, Taureans can find their way into jobs that would apply more to the signs of Aries or Scorpio, such as police work or careers in the armed forces.

Taurus and Money

Taureans don't usually start out rich and it may take them quite a while to build up any form of security. If they go into business for themselves, they may not make much money because few of them are true entrepreneurs, and they don't have the energy or the hunting instincts of a good salesperson. They do better by staying in a job and getting a pension at the end of it. Taureans make shrewd investments, hold on to what they have and gradually build up a good financial base, ending their lives in some measure of comfort. Some Taureans are not too proud to live off a wealthier partner. They are not interested in gambling and they rarely spend real money on gadgets or unnecessary items, because they prefer to save up or wait for something worth having. They will only lay out for "extras" once the basic household bills have been covered and there is some spare money in the bank for emergencies. If hard times come, they work hard to get back on their feet.

Taurus Relationships

Taureans are true family people and they don't usually go in for affairs and adventures, but despite this, some are surprisingly flirtatious. If they are happy in their first marriage they stick to their partner for life, but if this doesn't work out they usually marry again sooner or later because they are sociable and they don't enjoy too much of their own company. Taureans remain close to their children and they make an effort to meet up with their adult offspring as often as possible even when their children live on the other side of the world. These people are loving and reliable partners who are for the most part calm and reasonable to live with. Their obstinacy can make them difficult, and sometimes they are so blinkered that they can't see any other way of doing things but their own. If it comes to a divorce, they will get so caught up in fighting over money or trying to impoverish their ex-partner that they do more damage to their families and themselves than they realize.

They take care of older relatives and they enjoy keeping in touch with other relatives. Many Taureans become dab hands at using the Internet to keep in touch with more distant relations. Their friendships rarely take precedence over their families.

Home Life

If there is one thing Taureans love it is their homes, and they will make the most humble of homes into a palace. Their homes are filled with comfortable furniture, art and pleasing objects. Taurean houses are likely to be tidy but there is often a collection of junk hidden away in the loft or the garage. A well-appointed kitchen is a must, because Taureans of both sexes like to cook and to entertain, but while they will buy good general equipment, they don't waste money needlessly on fancy gadgets. Another important factor for these subjects is a garden. Taureans are not apartment dwellers, they like to see a bit of land around their home and they are clever cultivators, often growing food for the table as well as flowers and attractive trees.

Taurus Health

Taurus is a particularly healthy sign and many Taureans live for a very long time. They don't drink too much and as long as they don't smoke or sit around too much they are usually pretty fit. Look at our Queen Elizabeth. She comes from a long-lived family and will doubtless live an exceptionally long life herself. In true Taurean fashion, she will probably hang on to her job and position even when she is long past doing any real work. Another example is Pope John Paul, who is still working despite his age and infirmities. The Taurus sore spot is the throat and neck, and the lower jaw. Most wear spectacles and some develop problems with the eyes. Most subjects have a sweet tooth, and even if they start out slim, they need to watch their weight later.

A Few Stray Facts

Even an apparently unconventional Taurean will usually end up living a conventional life. I have one young friend who is gay, but she is living in a happy relationship with a really lovely young woman. They are buying their flat and their great love is their two dogs, which they refer to as their "children".

Taureans enjoy traveling in comfort and they dislike roughing it, so cruises and good hotels appeal to them, rather than camping or backpacking.

You won't find this mentioned in any astrology book, but Taureans are natural counselors, so if you have a problem that you need to talk over with a wise, sympathetic and trustworthy friend, call a Taurus. However, once you have done this, don't keep going back for more, because they can get bored.

Taurus Decans

The first Decan is also Taurus, but the second is Virgo and the third is Capricorn. Read through the brief descriptions below and then turn to the chapters on Virgo and Capricorn for more.

1st Decan, Taurus

Pure Taurus. The chief problem is obstinacy and fixed opinions or an inability to change or to go with the flow. Taurean blessings are a kind heart and artistic or creative talent. These sensible and reliable subjects rarely do anything truly stupid. Family, friends and even household pets are of supreme importance to them. They are thorough and responsible but they cannot be rushed.

2nd Decan, Virgo

The Virgo influence adds intellect and a more academic mind than the other types. There may be an interest in research or analysis. This can also make the Taurean fussy about food, the appearance of his home or the way he works. The Virgoan slant makes this type more self-critical and self-sacrificial than the others.

3rd Decan, Capricorn

The Capricorn influence adds a fondness for family life and a close attachment to the parents. This type is more ambitious than the others, which, combined with thoroughness, caution over financial matters and a good business mind, can make them extremely successful. They are inclined to take offence easily and to be fussy about minor matters.

Taurus Dwaads

The first Dwaad is Taurus, so no change here. For all other Dwaads, read the chapter on the sign in question and also the brief description given below to see what adjustments or additions are made to the original sign.

Sign	What is added
Taurus	Pure Taurus.
Gemini	Quickness of mind, an inclination to worry, versatility, friendliness.
Cancer	Love of home and family, love of travel and the sea, business acumen.
Leo	Generosity, high personal standards, love of luxury and of children.
Virgo	Intellect, thoroughness, love of research. Can be critical or self-critical.
Libra	Love of luxury, friendliness, laziness. Desire for justice.
Scorpio	Interest in military, medical or police type matters, can be resentful.
Sagittarius	Humor, restlessness, technical skill, adventurousness, need for freedom.
Capricorn	Ambition, love of family, caution with money, business acumen.
Aquarius	Originality, humor, independence, friendliness, obstinacy.
Pisces	Love of art and music, spirituality, travel, interest in spirituality.
Aries	Courage, adventurousness, outgoing personality, love of music.

Sun Sign Gemini

May 21 to June 20
Ruling planet: Mercury
Symbol: The Twins
Gender: Masculine
This indicates an extrovert, active, courageous and somewhat
pushy manner.

The Element of Air
Gemini, Libra, Aquarius

The air sign mind is always active. Whether they are humming tunes in their head or playing out ideas and daydreams, their brains are rarely still. Many of them are sociable and friendly and their homes may be filled with neighbors, friends and relatives who pop in or stay for a night or two. Many are good at crafts, handiwork and mechanical tasks, and most seem to be able to cope very well with household tasks such as decorating or do-it-themselves jobs. Some love to collect tools, equipment or gadgets. They come up with wonderfully inventive answers to other people's problems, although they can find it hard to solve their own. They are excellent communicators and they may spend hours on the phone or the computer. They can be restless and tenser than they appear and they need a mildly sporting outlet or a change of scene on occasion to help them keep a healthy balance. Many are excellent teachers.

Air sign people are sympathetic to the plight of others, although they aren't good at shouldering the burdens of others for too long as this wears down their own delicate nervous systems. They may seek to protect their sensitive nerves by behaving in a way that is critical or unfeeling towards those who are close to them. Most air sign people are hopeless with those who are sick and they may lack patience with family members who become ill or downhearted. Air sign people can touch with reality, either by worrying about things that are not important or by living in a kind of fantasy-land.

The Mutable Quality
Gemini, Virgo, Sagittarius, Pisces

Mutable signs need variety and change and this may take them into careers, which ensure that each day is different from the next. Some prefer the kind of job that takes them from one place to another, while others travel far afield. Many work in one place, but deal with a variety of people or tasks during the course of each day. Mutable sign people may choose unconventional jobs or lifestyles because it is more important for their work to fit in with their beliefs or to fulfil their spiritual needs. Many work in fields that either expand people's minds, such as writing or publishing, while others work in fields that expand their experiences, such as the travel trade or psychic work. These people sometimes choose to work in jobs that improve the lot of others, even though they can't earn much or climb the ladder of material success this way. There is a streak of independence and unconventionality about all the mutable signs, although this is less obvious in Gemini and Virgo, than it is in Sagittarius and Pisces. Many mutable sign types marry when young and start their families early. However, these early relationships all too frequently break up and they may go through a period of experimentation with a variety of partners before settling down again.

Gemini Looks

Most Geminis are average height or a little less, and they are inclined to be slim - sometimes even too thin but some Geminis are extremely overweight, so there doesn't seem to be much of a happy medium. Some start out extremely thin and become large later in life, others go from thin to positively scrawny later in life. There is no specific hair color for this sign but those from white races tend to have fair skins. Many Geminis have long necks. Geminis take a good deal of care about their appearance and they can remain young looking until well into old age. Many Geminis have very fine hair, which is terrific if there is plenty of it but some have such sparse hair that becomes the bane of their lives.

Main Characteristics

Geminis are kindly, friendly, sociable and great company. These intelligent up-to-date people are sympathetic listeners and easy talkers and they are wonderful to have as friends. These admirable people are rarely lazy, and even quite sickly Geminis hold down jobs. They value family life, but they can alienate their children by being unduly bossy parents. If they lose out in love, it almost destroys them and they take a long time to get over it.

General Character

When Geminis discover that I am interested in astrology, they often rush to point out that they consider themselves to be two-sided, like their symbol, the Twins. I honestly can't see that they are any more double or multi-faceted than any other sign, but I guess they know what they mean. What I do know is that Geminis are often restless and dissatisfied with their lives and some are constantly on the hunt for something better. In some cases, this takes them into one marriage after another; in others it takes them from job to job or place to place. Others stay put but become complainers and bores, allowing that typical Gemini whine to enter their voices when focusing on their favorite subject - themselves! They do have a point though, because

Geminis often go through a difficult childhood and a disappointing early marriage before hitting their stride later in life. For them, life truly does begin at forty and then improves as each succeeding year passes by. Geminis crave security, but they can find it stifling and while they love change and variety, if there is too much of it they feel insecure.

Geminis are friendly, sociable and good company. They enjoy eating and drinking with friends and relatives, and they love an opportunity to have a good laugh, but they can be relied upon not to become loud or to make an exhibition of themselves. Geminis have a reputation for not being able to stick to anything for long, but this is not really the case. They are happy to study or work at something that interests them and they only switch off when they are bored, but they can't stick to a repetitive routine or take on a large job that requires concentration on details. All the Geminis that I have come across need jobs and lifestyles that include variety and novelty. Geminis can't listen to those who tell long-winded stories, and when confronted by a bore they switch off and change the subject. Some may have butterfly minds, but others can study hard as long as they find the subject interesting.

The downside of this sign is a tendency to worry and to cross bridges before they come to them. Some Geminis become obsessed with past hurts, and when a marriage or a love affair goes wrong, it can take them many years to put it behind them and to move on. Sometimes their brain refuses to switch off, so that they end up running on nervous energy and tiring themselves out. They enjoy their own company but they like to know that their friends and relatives are on the end of the phone. Geminis are quick thinking, humorous, kindhearted and generous. More manipulative types of people can take advantage of their generosity and good hearts. The fact is that the vast majority of Geminis are co-operative, reasonable, responsible, hard working and easy to get along with, which is why they are so much in demand both at work and socially.

Gemini Careers

Geminis need variety in their work and also contact with a variety of different people. They often opt for a job where they meet or deal with new people on a frequent basis. Some are happy to stay in one place as long as they have the variety of tasks and people to deal with, while others like to get around and have constant changes of scene. Many choose to work in some form of business, often working for large organizations. Clerical work, telephone work and public relations are favorite Gemini careers, while others find work as chauffeurs or taxi drivers. Many Geminis find work in the fields of accountancy and banking and they have a natural affinity with figures. I remember one Gemini who worked in a bank commenting to me that eight of the nine accountants working there were also Geminis.

Other natural fields for Geminis are teaching, broadcasting and journalism. Many Geminis are more attuned to young people than older ones, so they enjoy helping out in youth or school activities. Many are musical or clever at some kind of craftwork, so they may take this up as part of their work or as a hobby. Some go into psychology or counseling.

Gemini and Money

These subjects are usually sensible where money is concerned, although they can overspend on clothes, especially accessories such as bags, belts and scarves. Females look good in colorful scarves and big earrings because their necks are rather long. Male Geminis will fill their wardrobes with expensive casual clothes and sporty outfits. Geminis have an uncanny knack of marrying those who earn good money and some Gemini ladies will even take on the role of "trophy wife" to a wealthy older man. When hard times come, they can cope with budgeting and cutting down, but for the most part they prefer to live in comfort. If nobody else is around to smooth their financial path, they go out and find ways of earning good money themselves.

Gemini Relationships

Geminis are relaters who prefer being in a partnership to being alone and they will go half way to meet almost any type of partner. They can irritate a partner by being moody, restless and inclined to go on about themselves and to fuss and worry about trifles, but for the most part they are perfectly reasonable. Geminis enjoy talking and listening, and their wit and humor makes them fun to be with. Geminis are not heavily into housework, but they will buy whatever gadgets they need to get the job done or they will find someone to do the chores for them so that their homes run smoothly. They won't complain to their partners if a meal is not up to scratch or if the place is temporarily untidy although most can't live in a real mess for long. These subjects need a bit of peace and quiet and time to themselves, even when their family lives are busy. Most love pottering around in the garden, as this practical outlet relaxes them. Geminis are flirtatious and while some are unreliable in relationships, others simply enjoy flirting and being admired by the opposite sex. Geminis can be quite highly sexed, and the dual nature of their personality means that many of them go through some period of their lives with more than one partner on the go at the same time.

One odd fact is that Geminis often find themselves involved with those who are in some way related to them, sometimes forming relationships with brothers-in-law or cousins. I have even come across circumstances where the Gemini has married a complete stranger, only to discover later that they are kin.

Gemini Home Life

It is always nice to visit a Gemini because his home is invariably comfortable. It is neither so tidy that it resembles an operating theatre nor so untidy that one feels unnerved by it. Most Geminis have an eye for color and decor, so their homes are quite stylish and a la mode. Having said this, these people don't make themselves slaves to housework. Geminis love company and they are happy to put the kettle on for tea, dig out a piece of cake and settle down for a good old gossip. Many Geminis marry more than once, so the chances are that various children, step-relatives and other parts of their extended families drop in fairly frequently. When not gossiping with friends and relatives in person, Geminis keep in touch with everybody on the phone and by email.

Gemini Health

Gemini weak spots are the lungs and also the hands, wrists, arms and shoulders. I have noticed that many Geminis suffer badly with their teeth. Their second teeth often need to be straightened and this can take years of expensive treatment either when they are teenagers or later in life. Gemini teeth fall apart easily and they can suffer badly with toothache or neuralgia, which is set off by dental problems. Some also suffer with eye problems. The worst health problem is general nervousness, which can lead to stress. In the old days, practically every Gemini smoked, but this is less so these days.

Some Geminis are real hypochondriacs who worry unduly about every little thing. Some run to the doctor at least once a week, others take every kind of alternative medicine that they can locate.

A Few Stray Facts

Geminis can be surprisingly bossy, and some insist on talking to their children as if they were stupid or naughty two-year-olds, even when the children are fully-grown. They can get into the habit of thinking they know best and letting those around them know it.

If Geminis play sports or games, they prefer single combat to team games. Their small light frames make them naturals for gymnastics, tennis, badminton and squash, while some can even get into less common things, such as training or showing dogs.

Many Geminis look after parents, grandparents and so on, either in a practical sense or by financing them in their old age.

Some Geminis are fussy eaters and many really don't like the activity of eating at all. I recently read a scientific study that said that the highest number of anorexic and bulimic people were born in May and June. The report suggested that this was probably because the pregnancy had occurred during the winter and that their mothers had suffered with influenza and other fevers during the early stages of pregnancy, which had some kind of effect on the brain chemistry. Whether this is true or not, it is a fact that many Geminis prefer a coffee and cigarette to a heavy meal.

Gemini Decans

The first Decan is also Gemini, but the second is Libra and the third is Aquarius. Read through the brief descriptions below and then turn to the chapters on Libra and Aquarius for more.

1st Decan, Gemini

Pure Gemini. Geminis grasp new concepts easily, but they get bored with them again very quickly. They are always in a hurry. This type of Gemini rarely has time for lame ducks or time-wasters. Family life is extremely important, but this doesn't stop them flirting. The duality of the sign means that they can alternate between being spendthrift to being extremely cautious about money.

2nd Decan Libra

Libra increases the interest in love and relationships; it also makes these Geminis determined to have things their own way and it can make them argumentative, sarcastic and cutting. The Libran influence can make this type extremely loving or demanding, apt to talk "at" people and go on about themselves, while others are great listeners, more interested in others than themselves. It all depends upon which twin or side of the scales rules the individual person. Libra brings a love of music, arts, fashion and beauty, which, allied to Geminian intelligence, can take some into careers or hobbies in these fields. This influence also endows a desire for justice and honesty, both in relationships and business dealings.

3rd Decan Aquarius

The Aquarian influence endows the Gemini with an offbeat sense of humor and interests in unusual subjects. These Geminis may have scientific minds, and they may be deeply interested in human behavior and psychology. They have original and independent minds, and a "different" approach to life. These subjects are less butterfly-minded than the other types, and they can study subjects that interest them quite deeply. Some are very attracted to the world of psychology, and they may take this up as a career.

Gemini Dwaads

The first Dwaad is Gemini, so no change here. For all other Dwaads, read the chapter on the sign in question and also the brief description given below to see what adjustments or additions are made to the original sign.

Sign	What it adds
Gemini	Pure Gemini.
Cancer	Love of family, caution, financial acumen, love of novelty.
Leo	Pride, love of luxury, beauty and music. Love of children, creativity.
Virgo	An academic mind, thoroughness, fussiness over health, food etc.
Libra	Love of luxury, interest in relationships, sociability, sexiness.
Scorpio	Interest in psychology, love of words or music, determination.
Sagittarius	Interest in teaching or studying, humor, love of travel.
Capricorn	Ambition, common sense, business acumen, love of family.
Aquarius	Interest in astrology or other philosophical subjects, originality.
Pisces	Flexibility, lack of money sense, sympathy, kindness, vulnerability.
Aries	Ambition, teaching ability, quickness of mind, witty and humorous.
Taurus	Talent for building, gardening, creative pursuits and less tension.

Sun Sign Cancer

June 21 to July 22
Ruling planet: The Moon
Symbol: The Crab
Gender: Feminine
Feminine sign types are introverts who are more thorough and patient than the masculine sign types. These types can put up with quite a lot of hardship.

The Water Group

Feminine
Cancer, Scorpio, Pisces

Water sign people respond slowly when asked a question and they turn round slowly when called. These people need time to grasp new ideas because they need to filter them through their feelings before they can make up their minds. Their feelings run deep and they can be very emotional. When upset, they sulk, brood and they can even be cruel towards those who are close to them. They are extremely intuitive, they sum people up accurately, and they tend to feel everything that is going on in the surrounding atmosphere. They use this knowledge to avoid falling into traps that others simply don't see. Water sign people can be attracted to the world of business where their shrewdness and good grasp of money-matters stands them in good stead. Trust is important to them and they prefer to ally themselves to those who they can trust and rely upon.

Water sign people can love very deeply, but some of them save their greatest love for their children or for animals. They keep sensitive feelings hidden, sometimes even from themselves, and this allows irritation and resentment to build up. Once this happens, they either fall into depression or explode - much to the surprise and hurt of those who are around them. Water sign people are restless and they like to get out and about with their work and their social life, they also love to travel and explore new places. Having said this, they also need a base, a secure home and an office, shop or workshop that they can call their own. Environments are important to them and too much noise or disturbance upsets them.

The Cardinal Quality
Aries, Cancer, Libra, Capricorn

Cardinal types don't let the grass grow under their feet and they are inclined to do what they think best for themselves, their family or their group. They can put themselves out to fit in with others, where necessary, but they can't leave their own needs too far out in the cold. When the chips are down they know that they can depend upon themselves. Once they have made their minds up (and this includes the vacillating sign of Libra), they can't be pushed from their path. Cardinal people take advantage of opportunities, they make the most of them and they can be good leaders as long as they allow others an opinion and an opportunity to use their creativity. One thing they are often good at is motivating and encouraging others, but they may then ask or expect too much of others. Despite the strength of this type, their confidence can evaporate and the need the support of a partner or at the very least a couple of good friends.

Cancerian Looks

There is a marked difference between those born with the Sun in Cancer to those with Cancer rising. The Cancer rising subject has a rounded body shape and characteristically chubby cheeks. The Sun-in-Cancer person is often slim and of medium height or a little taller, with strongly marked features and an expressive face. Many Cancerians have lines on their foreheads from quite a young age, and they can become quite lined and craggy looking in later life. Think of Harrison Ford, or what Tom Cruise might look like in later life. Cancerians have a ready smile, which accompanies their wonderful sense of humor. If they can keep their sweet tooth under control, these subjects remain reasonably slim; otherwise they can become overweight. Most Cancerians have quite thick hair and the men keep much of their hair as they grow older. Some have extremely sensitive skin and the men are prone to "razor-rash", therefore many Cancerian men give up on the idea of shaving and sport a beard instead.

Main Characteristics

Cancerians need a base, preferably a fully paid-up mortgage and a small business. They don't necessarily want to stay indoors very much as they enjoy getting out and about and traveling, but they definitely need a place to come home to. They love their families and they try to maintain good relationships with all generations within the group. Cancerians can be crabby and moody at times and some can be extreme bullies who use their considerable intuition to press other people's buttons or degrade those who they consider a threat. One rather unpleasant aspect of their character is that far too often they victimize the wrong person, choosing to make a victim out of the one person who doesn't pose a threat and who has no escape route.

General Character

Cancerians are so friendly that they have many acquaintances, but only those whom they really trust are allowed to get really close to them. They are cautious, slightly introverted and happiest when among family members or with their very few real friends. Cancerians are extremely loyal to their families and they will do everything in their power to look after them. Sometimes this is taken to extremes and they find it especially difficult to let go when their growing children become independent. They do all they can to help their parents when they get older.

Cancerians need base, a home and sometimes also a business that they can call their own and that they can retreat to. A room of their own or a corner of the house to themselves are also sometimes necessary. Having said this, they love to travel, to visit friends and go out to events in their locality. These people are not big spenders and they always try to put something by for a rainy day. Cancerians have a natural aptitude for business and for dealing with the public, but they are usually too shy to put themselves on display or address an audience. They do best in business when linked with a more adventurous partner. Cancerians love things that have some kind of history attached to them, or that have a sentimental value for them, so they may deal in these things or become collectors.

Cancer is a water sign, which means that they often react slowly to events. If you call out to these people, they turn round slowly or take time to answer. They filter everything through their emotions and their reaction to everything tends to be emotional rather than strictly rational. They can get upset over nothing, or take a casual remark as an insult and they can become moody, depressed, self-pitying or sarcastic and confrontational. The other side to this coin is that they sympathize readily with the plight of others. They are kind hearted and sympathetic and they have a rare talent for really listening to what others are saying. They are loyal to those who are good to them, they take responsibility well and they can make the very best of friends, relatives and colleagues at work.

Career

Cancerians are drawn to the idea of having a business of their own and they have a knack for providing the goods and services that the public wants or needs. Therefore, these subjects often end up with a small business, or a shop that provides useful goods or specialized services. Property and real estate fascinate many and others are interested in insurance, so these are fields that can attract them. Many enjoy working with small children, so Cancerian women with small children of their own may turn being at home with them an advantage by making a living out of looking after people's children in addition to their own. Some Cancerians teach, often specializing in financial subjects, geography or history. Others work in banking or business, especially export or anything else with a foreign connection. A few find their way into the armed forces, especially the navy. Their attachment to the sea can take them into careers in the merchant navy, fishing or on a cruise liner.

Cancer and Money

Cancerians are cautious and they like to have something behind them to fall back on, so they save for the future. Their entrepreneurial instincts often take them into business where their intuition and feelings about people and trends can be very helpful, but this can work against them, as there are times when a cool and logical attitude would suit them better. Cancerians rarely waste money on gadgets or unnecessary items, but they ensure that they have the equipment they need for their work or their homes. If they can afford to do so, they spend quite freely on travel.

Home is Where the Cancerian Heart is

Many Cancerians work from home and they love to be surrounded by their families and to have friends dropping in. If the Cancerian spends at all freely, it is on the household, the family and on home comforts. A comfortable and attractive home is a must for these people but they rarely turn this into a show place or behave obsessively about decor or tidiness. The Cancerian home is a pleasant, comfortable and welcoming place. These subjects love entertaining and most are excellent cooks. Some go in for old-fashioned skills such as jam making, bottling fruit and making relishes or chutneys and they enjoy baking bread and cakes, so the first thing that hits a visitor to a Cancerian home is the delicious smell emanating from the kitchen. Most Cancerians collect a great deal of junk during their lifetimes, so they need plenty of loft space, cupboard space and a garage or two to keep it all in.

Cancerian Relationships

Many Cancerian relationships have some element of parenting in them. Some take on the role of parent to a partner, while others look for someone who will mother them. Most Cancerians have children of their own and also pets to care for.

Apart from these considerations, most Cancerians like being married and they enjoy family life. If this goes wrong, they can live alone for a while, but they are social creatures who like getting out and about; sooner or later, they will find themselves a new partner. Some Cancerians are so difficult to live with that they kill off potential partnerships almost before they start, but others bring their kindness, their caring nature and a wonderful sense of fun to their relationships. It takes a lot for these people to give up on a relationship or even to admit to themselves that it is no longer viable.

Health

The word cancer is so feared that at one point in time, American astrologers used the term "Moon child" to represent this sign. I have known Cancerian people who have suffered from cancer and others who have not and I have known plenty of people from other signs of the zodiac who have gone down with this disease. However, it is slightly more prevalent in this sign than in others. Therefore, if you are a Cancerian and you feel that there is something wrong with you, do check it out, if only to put your mind at rest. A more likely scenario for this watery sign is rheumatism or arthritis. Colds turn to bronchitis, especially when the Cancerian is under stress. Having said all the above, this is not an especially sickly sign and young Cancerians suffer far less illness than children of other signs.

A Few stray Facts

Most Cancerians love the sea and ships and all appreciate holidays near or on water.

Most of these subjects enjoy looking after small animals, especially if their children like them.

Cancerians rarely drink much alcohol, and if they drink at all they prefer quality wines and spirits. Their downfall is their sweet tooth, which means that they are much more likely to overdo things with chocolate cake than with booze.

These people can get themselves in a state over nothing, especially if they have planets in nearby Gemini.

Cancerians love nothing better than a good old gossip with their friends or family, and their phone bills are at least as heavy as those of any other sign of the zodiac. They rarely give up on their friends.

Cancer Decans

The first Decan is also Cancer, but the second is Scorpio and the third Pisces. Read through the brief descriptions below and then turn to the chapters on Scorpio and Pisces for more.

1st Decan, Cancer

Pure Cancer. Home is where the Cancerian heart is and the family means a great deal to these people but they do need to escape from time to time. Cancerians enjoy short trips and outings, novelty, eating out and seeing new faces and places. They can switch from being the most sympathetic listener to being moody, crabby and cantankerous.

2nd Decan, Scorpio

The Scorpio influence adds depth to the emotions and it can unfortunately add a sharp tongue and unnecessary feelings of resentment. These people make excellent researchers and their high level of intuition can make them quite psychic. They are extremely patriotic, which means that they may become experts in the history of their country (especially the military history).

3rd Decan, Pisces

This adds mysticism, intuition, imagination and psychism to the Cancerian character. I have one friend who has put her strong imagination to good use by writing books for children. This adds a creative, artistic and sensitive streak. These types can be a bit defensive. They are far less money-minded than the other two types and less inclined to make a success of a business enterprise.

Cancer Dwaads

The first Dwaad is Cancer, so no change here. For all other Dwaads, read the chapter on the sign in question and also the brief descriptions given below to see what adjustments or additions are made to the original sign.

Sign	What is added
Cancer	Pure Cancer.
Leo	Adds confidence, obstinacy, love of drama and a steadfast nature.
Virgo	Adds intellect, quickness, an eye for detail, an interest in food and health.
Libra	This can make the nature volatile. Unsettled love relationships.
Scorpio	A deeply emotional type who is also strongly intuitive.
Sagittarius	Confusing mix of a need to cling and to be free. Good actor, traveler.
Capricorn	A tycoon with a head for big business. Close to parents and family.
Aquarius	Has great ideas for home improvements. Inventive imagination.
Pisces	Imaginative, musical, artistic, creative, somewhat impractical.
Aries	A determined and bossy personality. Great sense of humor, intelligent.
Taurus	Home loving, a little domineering. Artistic around the home and garden.
Gemini	Switches from peaceful to nervy and jumpy. Home loving, friendly.

Sun Sign Leo

July 23 to August 22
Ruling planet: The Sun
Symbol: The Lion
Gender: Masculine
This indicates an extrovert, active, courageous and somewhat pushy nature.

The Element of Fire
Aries, Leo, Sagittarius

Fire sign people do things quickly and they don't allow the grass to grow under their feet. They may commit themselves to a course of action and then regret it, because they haven't given themselves enough time to think things through. On the other hand, while others are procrastinating and putting off unpleasant chores or simply not getting their act together, the fire signs are well on the way to finishing the job. Fire people display initiative, courage and leadership qualities. Some are genuinely selfish; while others are so quick to think and act that they leave others behind in their haste to get on with things. Despite their apparent selfishness, many are idealists who really do want to make the world a better place.

Fire sign people have no patience with those who hesitate, and they don't understand that it is not necessarily someone else's karma to grasp every opportunity that comes along. These subjects are quick, intelligent, humorous and generous, and they love their friends and family. They become angry when others oppose them, irritable when they are tired or hungry, and they can be extremely cutting when they are wound up, but they rarely sulk. They need a good standard of living to keep up with their spending habits. Fire sign people are often passionate lovers who live life to the full.

Fire sign people are less confident than they appear; they can suddenly lose faith in themselves and become depressed when too much goes wrong. They need a steady and reliable partner who will respect them for their undoubted talents and who doesn't seek to undermine them. In turn, fire sign people need to be reminded to validate their partner and not to build up their own ego at the expense of others.

Fire sign people are often worryingly underweight as children, but they soon get over this and they can become quite heavy later in life.

The Fixed Quality
Taurus, Leo, Scorpio, Aquarius

Fixed people try to maintain the status quo and most prefer a well-ordered life, because too much change makes them uncomfortable. Taureans, Leos and Scorpios need financial security and they fear getting into debt, but Aquarians are less concerned about this. A happy relationship and emotional security are important to these people, and they try to work out the problems within a relationship, if at all possible, rather than giving up at the first hurdle. All fixed sign people are obstinate, which may make their life and the lives of those around them difficult in some ways. However, this trait comes to every one's aid when they take on a large task; they do it thoroughly and see it through to a conclusion. Fixed sign people can put up with boredom and repetition if a job requires it, but outside of work, they enjoy change and novelty as much as any other type. They have a responsible attitude to life and they take their duties seriously.

Looks

Leos are pretty good-looking as a whole, and Leo women can be quite spectacular with their characteristically thick mane of hair. Male Leos will become a little thin on top later in life, while the females keep their thick and bouncy hair throughout life. Leos are normally of middle height and even a little short in some cases, but they hold themselves well and they have the kind of presence that makes it hard to overlook them. Both sexes are likely to be underweight as children, filling out at puberty and then putting on weight in middle age, especially round the abdomen. Leos are not fond of exercise, so becoming overweight can be a problem to them, but their vanity means that they will take themselves in hand if necessary. When Leos have money to spare, they spend it on their appearance.

Main Characteristics

Leos have high standards and they prefer a comfortable and moneyed lifestyle. They are usually close to their family, but their greatest love is their children. Leos are hard workers who frequently run their own businesses. They can be bossy, very self-centered and they tend to lay down the law to others, but they are bighearted, generous and they mean well.

General Character

Leos love their families, and if they have loving parents, they will remain close to them throughout life. If their parents are not good to them, they try to create a happy family for themselves through marriage and parenthood. Leos adore their children, they spoil them and love them to bits, but they won't stand any nonsense from them and they try to instill good behavior and self-respect. These subjects are usually extremely generous to their relatives, but they are not especially charitable to outsiders, and they can be quite devious or demanding when it comes to their business dealings. Leos are hard workers, often self-made men or women, and they have little patience with those who are worse off than themselves. They have even less time for suffering humanity, which makes them less charitable than other zodiac signs.

Despite their occasional lapses, Leos are proud and like to be thought of as having integrity. They can also become extremely irritable and unreasonable when they are pressured, fatigued or hungry. Leos can panic when under pressure, but after the initial attack of nerves has passed, they take control of the situation and demonstrate their wonderful leadership qualities. These subjects have extremely high standards and they can expect far too much of themselves and of others. This can lead to disappointment or even depression at times. Although generally self-confident and somewhat arrogant, Leos can suddenly find that their confidence evaporates and that they need a sympathetic friend to prop them up, but their natural optimism means that they generally bounce back sooner or later.

Being a fixed sign, Leos prefer to stay in the same home and with the same partner for as long as possible, and they also remain in the same job as long as possible. When they have to make a change, they do so quite suddenly, although only after a long period of internal agonizing and analysis. Leos are pretty trusting souls, which means that they can be hurt or badly used. They have long memories for those who help them and also for those who hurt them, and they definitely hold grudges. They are extremely loyal to their friends, relatives and colleagues. Some Leos have such an eye on the main chance that they will push others out of the way in order to get where they need to be. Others are quite the opposite, being utterly honest both in matters of love and in the workplace. It is always wise to size up any Leo, to see which type they are before becoming too embroiled with them, as they can be either angels or devils.

Leo Careers

There are many career paths that attract Leos, but the most common is some form of fast-moving business. If this gives them the opportunity to travel or to deal with upmarket, up-to-date products or something glamorous and exciting, so much the better. Leos feel most at home when running the show, so you can find them working as managers of large concerns, admin managers or perhaps running their own business. You can find Leos in broadcasting, publishing, public relations and the world of computers. Leos take to computing remarkably quickly, possibly because this is an easy way to handle large projects.

According to traditional astrology, one Leo career is the jewelry trade, but to be honest, I can't say that I have come across many Leos in this business. Show business is another matter, as is the glamour end of the fashion world. Some work in finance and others in the travel trade. Despite the fact that they are not drawn to down and out types, they can work hard for some form of upmarket charity organization, especially if it gives them an opportunity to put on large and glamorous events. The most important factor is that Leos are most comfortable when in charge of a project, as they are extremely capable and they have excellent organizational skills. They have the knack of picking staff that are as enthusiastic as they are about a project, and who pull their weight. In turn, Leos look after their subordinates, so they frequently inspire an almost devoted following. Most Leos love being in the limelight, either by being at the top of their careers or by working in the media, but there are plenty who write for a living and who work - at least on a part-time basis - as astrologers and occasionally also as clairvoyants.

Some rogue Leos are incredibly lazy and childish, while others are demanding, selfish and dishonest - none of which endears them to others or helps their career prospects - but the vast majority are hardworking and decent.

Leos and Money

Leos are spenders and they loathe being without money or in debt. Being sensible, Leos tend to set up independent savings schemes that remove money from their bank on a regular basis before their spendthrift habits or their generosity is able to kick in. These subjects are perfectly well aware that in good times, they can forget that things can go wrong and that their wealth can suddenly evaporate, so they try to curb their instincts and save. Leos can live on very little if they have to, but they don't enjoy it much. If they do get into financial difficulties, they find ways of earning their way out of trouble. Leos enjoy large, well-appointed houses and an appropriately gracious lifestyle. Given the opportunity, they entertain in style, send their children to fee-paying schools, take vacations in the nicest places and belong to all the best clubs.

Oddly enough, for such a generous sign, Leos don't like being owed money, and they will chase up debts. This doesn't please those who have a casual attitude to such things, or those who feel that the Leo has enough money already and doesn't need his loan repaid, or the goods and services that he provided to be paid for. Be aware - Leos always follow up on debts.

Home is Where the Children are

Most Leos live in houses, preferably those that are somewhat out of town and with a fair bit of land around them. When they do live in a city, they often live upstairs where they have a good view. I don't think any Leo could stand living in a basement apartment for long. Their homes are comfortable, well appointed and reasonably tidy, but some Leos go in for too much over-stuffed furniture and too many knick-knacks and other unnecessary features. Leos like art and music, so the chances are that they have attractive pictures on their walls and a good sound system. Most Leo homes are filled with children or animals. They love to entertain, although they won't kill themselves in the kitchen, so they often invite a crowd of friends and relatives round and then send for a take-out.

Leo Relationships

Leos don't like living alone. If they are happy being at home with their parents, they will delay marriage and partnerships but most will move in with someone or marry when young. Once a Leo has settled down, he will usually set about producing children pretty quickly. Leos who do not have children keep dogs, horses and other animals, which they treat as children. These fixed sign subjects will keep on trying to make a marriage work even against the odds, and they then become extremely upset if they have to call a halt - especially if there are children involved. Stupid situations sometimes arise, such as a couple breaking up but remaining under the same roof. Leos don't understand commitment phobia and they don't understand lovers who will take full advantage of their loving and generous natures, only to leave them in the lurch or to mess them around. They will give a lover a lot of rope, but sooner or later they move on and find a more reliable partner.

One strange phenomenon that seems to go against all that is usually said about this highly motivated and highly successful zodiac sign, is that they can be badly undermined by a marriage-type partner. Leos marry for love and try to stay in love, even when their partner is not actually all that lovable. They need to be loved, and worse still they will do all they can to be approved of and well thought of, so they try very hard in their marriages. They pour in enough love for both partners in the hope that this will make things come right, and it takes them a long time before they realize that they can't turn a sow's ear into a silk purse. After kidding themselves and their partners for years that they are satisfied with their situation, they suddenly wake up and take off, leaving the partner to wonder what went wrong.

Health

The sign of Leo rules the heart and spine. Being an energetic "A" type personality, this fire sign type can suffer from heart problems. Backache is almost par for the course for Leos at some time in their lives, but the neck and upper spine area is as likely to cause them problems as the more common lumbar region. Fevers, headaches and sudden infections are possible, but these usually clear away as quickly as they arrive. Leos tend to remain at work even when they fall ill, which doesn't help matters.

A Few Stray Facts

Leos don't enjoy taking exercise but they hate losing their figures so they will tend to join luxurious health clubs and so forth. One exercise that they do enjoy is swimming (as long as the water in the pool is bath-water warm), and they are often surprisingly good swimmers.

Most Leos can't throw or catch a ball for toffee and hitting it with any kind of bat or stick is often quite out of the question. If success depends on a Leo school child being good at baseball or something of the sort, he will either work at it until he achieves a passable level of success or he will find another avenue. Team games appeal even less to the average Leo than ball sports.

Leos have natural rhythm and they have the kind of spatial mind that can pick up and retain the patterns needed for dance steps, so many of them are a wow on the dance floor.

Many Leos loathe their schooldays and they may do very badly there, but they inevitably take extra courses at some later date, then catch up with their more successful peers and surpass them.

Leos love holidays and things that appeal to children, such as Disney World, are great favorites.

Leo Decans

The first Decan is also Leo, but the second is Sagittarius and the third is Aries. Read through the brief descriptions below and then turn to the chapters on Sagittarius and Aries for more.

First Decan, Leo

Pure Leo. These people have high standards and a great deal of pride, which means that they only accept the best from themselves. They cannot understand those who don't grasp opportunities when they come along, and they have no patience with those who they see as losers. They are loving, affectionate and sexy, and they love to be in love, but above all they adore their children.

Second Decan, Sagittarius

The Sagittarian influence adds flightiness and restlessness and it reduces the level of personal ambition. These people are more likely seek out jobs that interest them, rather than those that pay well or give them a terrific career path, and they will be less reliable in relationships than the other two Decan types. There may be a spiritual attitude to life or an interest in travel.

Third Decan, Aries

These Leos can be real go-getters and they are far more likely to initiate new ideas than the other two Decan types. They are more able to work as part of a team than the others, but they are happiest when organizing others. Even if they don't seek out this kind of responsibility, they always seem to have it thrust upon them. They enjoy outings and social life and traveling in comfort.

Leo Dwaads

The first Dwaad is also Leo, so no change here. For all other Dwaads, read the chapter on the sign in question and also the brief descriptions given below to see what adjustments are made to the original sign.

Sign	What is added
Leo	Pure Leo.
Virgo	A capacity for dealing with details, verbosity and hypochondria.
Libra	Sociability, an attachment to abstract ideas, sexuality, love of justice.
Scorpio	Sexuality, depth of thought and feeling. Intuition, caution.
Sagittarius	Humor and fun, originality, a gift for arts and crafts or building.
Capricorn	This makes an ambitious and capable business leader.
Aquarius	Originality, quirkiness, humor, an ability to think in the abstract.
Pisces	Makes the Leo artistic and musical, and adds spirituality.
Aries	Irritability and a tendency to argue. Also courage.
Taurus	Stamina, thoroughness. A quieter and less domineering personality.
Gemini	Intelligence, nervousness, a talkative nature, good organization skills.
Cancer	Love of home, security, cooking, family and social life, also travel.

Sun Sign Virgo

August 23 to September 22
Ruling planet: Mercury
Symbol: The Maiden
Gender: Feminine
Feminine sign types are introverts who are more thorough and patient than the masculine sign types. These types can put up with quite a lot of hardship.

The Element of Earth
Virgo, Capricorn, Taurus

These are practical, diligent and hardworking people who are happiest when they are doing something useful. They can be relied upon, and even though it might take them a while to get around to things, they usually get there in the end. These people are more ambitious than they appear and they may be shrewd operators in politics or in business. Their drawbacks are sometimes a lack of speed when action is needed, stubbornness, greed and distaste for chancy ventures or of spending money unnecessarily.

Most earth sign people are family types who need the security of a good relationship. They rarely walk away from family responsibility, even when family members are difficult to cope with. These subjects are sensual and loving, especially in a relationship that is comfortable and that gives them confidence. They may have a creative streak, although this manifests itself in different ways for each sign. Shrewd and cautious, they need material and emotional security and they can put up with a lot in order to get it. Many earth types appear tight-fisted, they can be shortsighted about financial matters and this is often due to a real or imagined fear of poverty.

The Mutable Quality
Gemini, Virgo, Sagittarius, Pisces

Mutable signs need variety and change and this may take them into careers, which ensure that each day is different from the next. Some prefer the kind of job that takes them from one place to another, while others travel far afield. Many work in one place, but deal with a variety of people or tasks during the course of each day. Mutable sign people may choose unconventional jobs or lifestyles because it is more important for their work to fit in with their beliefs or to fulfil their spiritual needs. Many work in fields that either expand people's minds, such as writing or publishing, while others work in fields that expand their experiences, such as the travel trade or psychic work. These people sometimes choose to work in jobs that improve the lot of others, even though they can't earn much or climb the ladder of material success this way. There is a streak of independence and unconventionality about all the mutable signs, although this is less obvious in Gemini and Virgo, than it is in Sagittarius and Pisces. Many mutable sign types marry when young and start their families early. However, these early relationships all too frequently break up and they may go through a period of experimentation with a variety of partners before settling down again.

Virgo Looks

Virgoans may have nothing more than average looks when young, and they consider a slim figure and regular features to be rather ordinary, but boy, do they cash in when they age! Some Virgoans get a little heavier in later life, but unless there is something else at work in their horoscopes, they usually remain in reasonable shape for their height. Their regular features and good bone structure ensure that their faces improve with age, rather than falling into folds or fatty lumps. Some Virgoans are a little angular and bony when young, but this makes them photogenic. The hair is fine but abundant, and often very dark or very pale in white races, so this too looks good throughout life. Many Virgoans have a distinct widow's peak hairline.

Main Characteristics

There is a pernickety side to all Virgoans, but each one expresses this differently. Some are fussy about their homes; others take trouble over their work or their appearance. Most accumulate knowledge about a particular subject and they can become experts in it. Although kindhearted, some can be extremely demanding and hard to live with. If they are let down in love, they take a very long time to get over it.

General Character

Virgoans are more comfortable with people who they know than with strangers and they either go to great lengths to charm outsiders, or alternatively to keep them at arm's length. Some can be prickly and off-putting on first acquaintance. These subjects are self-conscious and they fear censure by others because they are sensitive and easily hurt. Their sharp minds and uncanny ability to see through others can make them seem a little daunting. The reality is that Virgoans are so kindhearted that they are apt to sacrifice themselves for the needs of those whom they love and they are the best and most reliable friends that one can choose to have.

This is a practical earth sign, which is allied to the intellectual brilliance of the planet, Mercury. Virgoans have the talent and persistence to study chosen subjects in depth and to become experts. The Virgo mind is logical, analytical and quick, and many are also excellent communicators who use their talent in their careers. Virgoans people need a measure of status in their jobs and lifestyles and they need the respect of others if they are also to develop self-respect. They like orderly lives with each component kept neatly in its pigeonhole. This emotional kind of pigeonholing doesn't necessarily mean that their homes are models of cleanliness (although some are). For one thing, they often collect too much stuff for total tidiness. Virgoans often work in what looks like a flurry of papers and mess, but they know exactly where everything is (most of the time) and they simply can't stand it when others fiddle about with what is on their desks or with their belongings. These somewhat tense people have high standards for themselves and sometimes for others as well. Most are wonderfully amusing companions whose ready wit and their ability to relate anecdotes and stories makes them great fun to be with.

Some Virgoans are fussy and neurotic and they can be faddy eaters, hypochondriacs or worriers. Some agonize about things that are highly unlikely to happen. Believe it or not, I have known Virgoans who lose sleep because they are convinced that one day, they will be eaten by a tiger or poisoned by their local water supply. Psychologists tell us that dreams and fears about being eaten by tigers are common, and that they stem from a fear that the person is only just managing to cope with life, and feel that at any moment it might spiral out of control. Virgoans are wonderful critics who can effortlessly discriminate between what is good and what isn't. Unfortunately, some of them use their critical faculties to hurt others, while practically all Virgoans are far too ready to criticize themselves.

Virgoan Careers

Study, analysis and communication are the core issues here. Most Virgoans prefer to work behind the scenes than out in the limelight. Many work in radio, television and as journalists, often dealing with news topics where their ability to think on their feet comes to their aid. They enjoy being of service to the community and their own hypochondria can take them into the fields of medicine or complimentary healing. Most like a job that gives them variety and that stretches their minds. Some are so inventive that they come up with wonderful designs for great new gadgets.

The attachment of this sign to the time of the harvest can take them into the food industry, and many are excellent cooks. The world of publishing is full of Virgo back room boys. Publishing requires a logical mind, a talent for spotting errors and the ability to concentrate for long hours, allied to writing ability and a knack, both for details and for handling many jobs at once. This sign is also good at keeping within a budget and weeding out projects that won't work. There is a creative side to the Virgoan, which simply will not allow him to be a cipher or spend his days doing mind-numbing jobs.

One really unusual career that seems to attract Virgoans is that of impresario. They enjoy putting on shows, events and happenings, and they can cope with this stress far better than the internal stress of their own nervous tension. Another surprisingly common Virgo career is acting. They can become a different kind of personality when playing a role, and many have a talent for mimicry. Add this to their aptitude for words, for learning scripts, their self-discipline and their good bone structure, and it is not hard to see why so many make a success of a stage or screen career.

Money Matters to Virgoans

Some Virgoans make a great deal of money in such fields as finance and business, but most are content to earn a living doing something that they enjoy. Virgoans may not earn a fortune, but they rarely get into debt. Like all earth signs, Virgoans are careful with money and their pride insists that they don't end up looking like losers. Virgoans spend freely on books, music, art and anything that provides them with information and a window on the world. This means that they splash out on digital satellite television, computers and telephone technology. Many buy computers, cameras and other gadgets when there is a practical or work-related reason to do so. They enjoy the cinema, theatre and local events and some enjoy competing in sports and games - although for many their choice is more likely to be chess or scrabble than football. Despite this, they like to own their homes, to have a bank account and always to keep something back for a rainy day.

Some people accuse Virgoans of meanness, but this is not really the case. Virgoans don't usually start life with a silver spoon in their mouths and they have to make their own way up. After years of managing on very little, they find it difficult to spend money needlessly. Also, if they are owed money, they like to have it repaid - a circumstance that doesn't please those who tend to be casual with other people's money.

Home is Where the Books are

A Virgo without overstuffed bookshelves is hardly worthy of the name! Some go in for computers, cameras and electronic equipment while others love a well-equipped kitchen filled with every conceivable gadget. Virgoans love company and they enjoy entertaining their friends. Some prefer to do this on a formal basis by giving tasteful dinner parties, with tables perfectly laid, complete with cut glass decanters and napkin rings, while others just love having their pals round for wine and pizza. Many enjoy gardening, especially growing salads and vegetables for the table. In this case, not only do they enjoy the combination of working in the fresh air, but they also benefit from the mental relaxation that this affords and the grounding contact with the soil. The fact that pure, clean, fresh organic produce ends up on the family table doesn't hurt either.

Virgo Relationships

Some Virgoans enjoy family life while others are far better off living alone. Those who do have families manage very well, as long as they don't allow their fussiness and lack of confidence to make them tiresome. Virgoans take a very responsible attitude to family life and they will put up with a great deal before considering leaving a relationship or abandoning children. They show love for the family by cooking nice meals, keeping the house neat and clean and by making the lives of those who are around them work like clockwork. For some, this dutiful, almost servant-like attitude takes the place of what they see as embarrassing displays of affection. Virgoans will spend as much as they can afford on giving their children books, extra lessons and extracurricular activities. They teach their children to paint, make things or collect and sort stamps.

Those who live alone don't usually start out that way, and they may even marry twice before realizing that they prefer their own company. However, they are rarely lonely as they have so many friends that either their home is filled with a permanent, floating social club or they are never at home. Many work from home and this can contribute to the number of people that pass through the place, plus the busy condition of their phones, faxes and emails. Virgo is a sensual earth sign and these subjects need plenty of sex in order to show love, appreciation, for fun and for relaxation.

Health

Some Virgoans worry unduly about their health, others take a far more relaxed attitude. The weak spots are the stomach and bowels, which means that such ailments as colitis or irritable bowel syndrome can strike them - especially when they are stressed. Virgoans can suffer from skin ailments, but these are more likely to be a reaction to something that has upset them or even a bacterial infection rather than lingering problems such as eczema. Virgo feet can give them hell as well, as the tendons in their feet and lower legs can be quite taut and easily irritated.

A Few Stray Facts

Despite the picture that is usually painted of Virgoans being workaholics, they can switch off and be extremely lazy at times. Sometimes this is due to a simple need for them to relax their tense nervous system and take time out.

Virgoans can be natty dressers. Their choice of wardrobe is never outrageous, but their clothes are of good quality and often very stylish. Some spend a lot of money on their appearance while others make themselves look great on a shoestring.

Most Virgoans write, but they are not the world's greatest letter writers; they prefer the telephone.

These people find it hard to spend money on holidays and indulgences, except when it is for the benefit of others.

Virgo Decans

The first Decan is also Virgo, but the second is Capricorn and the third Taurus. Read through the brief descriptions below and then turn to the chapters on Capricorn and Taurus for more.

1st Decan, Virgo

Pure Virgo. The Virgo's working life may take precedence over pastimes and vacations, but friendship is also important. These subjects love to have fun with friends whenever they can tear themselves away from work. They are practical and capable, and they manage to run all the various compartments of their lives efficiently - most of the time. Many are happier living alone with lots of friends dropping in than being in a one-to-one partnership.

2nd Decan, Capricorn

The Capricorn influence may not do the Virgo any favors as this increases the fussiness of this sign. This person can handle any amount of details and he will have a real talent for both words and for scientific or engineering projects. Relationships may suffer or the person himself may suffer until he learns to lighten up. A dry sense of humor may save him from being a real pain, but his ambitious nature doesn't make him easy to live with.

3rd Decan, Taurus

The softer addition of the Taurus Decan helps this sign to enjoy life and to be less self-sacrificial or self-critical. These people have a real talent for creating beauty in the home or the garden and they can succeed in such things as singing, dancing, acting or something artistic. A touch of showbiz glamour is added here. These Virgoans love to eat out and to entertain and they a great head for money.

Virgo Dwaads

The first Dwaad is also Virgo, so no change here. For all other Dwaads, read the chapter on the sign in question and also the brief descriptions given below to see what adjustments are made to the original sign.

Sign	What is added
Virgo	Pure Virgo.
Libra	Talent for gardening, homemaking. Less driven, more indulgent nature.
Scorpio	Competitiveness, good business skills, suspicious attitude, thoroughness.
Sagittarius	Humor, talent for work as electrician, carpenter, engineer etc.
Capricorn	Ambition, fussiness, good head for science, math, details and business.
Aquarius	Originality, wordiness, love of gadgetry, teaching ability.
Pisces	Interest in medicine, health, tendency towards self-sacrifice.
Aries	Confidence, self-motivation, desire for justice, stronger personality.
Taurus	Practicality, craftsmanship, love of beauty, sensuality, laziness.
Gemini	Intelligence, quickness, nervousness and a tendency to worry.
Cancer	Love of home and family, need for financial and emotional security.
Leo	More desire to take charge of events and to be in the limelight.

Sun Sign Libra

September 23 to October 22
Ruling planet: Venus
Symbol: The Scales
Gender: Masculine
This indicates an extrovert, active, courageous and somewhat pushy manner.

The Element of Air
Gemini, Libra, Aquarius

The air sign mind is always active. Whether they are humming tunes in their head or playing out ideas and daydreams, their brains are rarely still. Many of them are sociable and friendly and their homes may be filled with neighbors, friends and relatives who pop in or stay for a night or two. Many are good at crafts, handiwork and mechanical tasks and most seem to be able to cope very well with household tasks such as decorating or do-it-themselves jobs. Some love to collect tools, equipment or gadgets. They come up with wonderfully inventive answers to other people's problems although they can find it hard to solve their own. They are excellent communicators and they may spend hours on the phone or the computer. They can be restless and tenser than they appear and they need a mildly sporting outlet or a change of scene on occasion to help them keep a healthy balance. Many are excellent teachers.

Air sign people are sympathetic to the plight of others, although they aren't good at shouldering the burdens of others for too long as this wears down their own delicate nervous systems. They may seek to protect their sensitive nerves by behaving in a way that is critical or unfeeling towards those who are close to them. Most air sign people are hopeless with those who are sick and they may lack patience with family members who become ill or downhearted. Air sign people can touch with reality, either by worrying about things that are not important or by living in a kind of fantasy-land.

The Cardinal Quality
Aries, Cancer, Libra, Capricorn

Cardinal types don't let the grass grow under their feet and they are inclined to do what they think best is for themselves, their family or their group. They can put themselves out to fit in with others, where necessary, but they can't leave their own needs too far out in the cold. When the chips are down but they know that they can depend upon themselves. Once they have made their minds up (and this includes the vacillating sign of Libra), they can't be pushed from their path. Cardinal people usually take advantage of opportunities, they make the most of them and they can be good leaders as long as they allow others an opinion and an opportunity to use their creativity. One thing they are often good at is motivating and encouraging others, but they may then ask or expect too much of others. Despite the strength of this type, their confidence can evaporate and they need the support of a partner or at the very least a couple of good friends.

Libran Looks

This is one of the best looking signs of the zodiac and many Librans have really lovely eyes, skin and hair. When they are smiling, their faces light up, but when they are angry, it is as though the sun has gone in. Most Librans are medium height and with a soft appearance that can become a little rounded later in life. They are vain about their looks, so they usually try to keep in shape. They also spend time and money on their hair and bodies and they always dress in an attractive and up-to-date manner.

Main Characteristics

Librans like being among people but some can be apt to talk "at" people and some are far too opinionated in a rather silly way. Others are intelligent and great at listening as well as talking. Librans are not particularly hard workers but they can get by as a result of falling into a job that suits them or finding a wealthy marriage partner. In theory, Librans hate injustice and if they can find the energy to do so, they can fight for a cause. Librans find it easy to attract the opposite sex and they are sexy and sensual. Some are extremely gentle and apt to give way or walk away when pushed, others stand their ground and can be extremely argumentative and aggressive.

General Character

Librans can be quite confusing because they come in so many different varieties. When one considers the facts, their sign is ruled by Venus, which is the most feminine of planets, but it is masculine and cardinal, and their symbol - the Scales - is the only inanimate object in the whole zodiac. No wonder they are sometimes muddled and indecisive, though many Librans make their minds up perfectly well as long as they are not rushed into doing so. Most Librans want to be liked, so they sometimes say what the other person wants to hear. Others prefer to disagree with everything that others say, almost on principle. In short, some are extremely soft and sweet, while others are extremely hard and sour.

Some Librans work hard, others are lazy. Some can think on their feet and others need time before they can get their act together. Most are successful in their careers. Sometimes it is charm that takes them to the top, while in other cases it is hard work and talent and in yet others, it is the ability to pick excellent partners and subordinates. Their chief fault is a lack of reality and a tendency to live in a dream world. Some are so idealistic that they lose touch with reality. Most Librans are kindhearted and generous with their time and their sympathy; they will put themselves out for others, but there are those who can't be bothered. In short, Librans vary.

All Librans have excellent taste and a real sense of style, so they always look great. Many are refined and slightly upper class in behavior, so they rarely act in a coarse or unpleasant manner. Librans have a strange form of in-built self-preservation that keeps them out of harm's way much of the time. Most also mean well and really do want to make others happy. Most are generous and good-hearted.

Libran Careers

Many Librans talk for a living. This can lead them into legal work, where their communication skills, smooth, urbane appearance and delivery, their fine minds and intrinsic sense of justice make them skilled and successful. Some work as agents or arbitrators, while others negotiate wonderful business deals. Those who choose more practical fields can be found in the fashion or cosmetics industry, sometimes manufacturing or selling these or working as make-up artists. Many drift into jobs connected with music, the fashion trade and anything related to the arts. Many are quite handy, so they will find work as carpenters or electricians, but they soon move up in an organization so that they can direct the work of others rather than having to do it themselves. They can be surprisingly lucky in their working life. Despite their charm, Librans don't make good salesmen, due perhaps to a lack of any real killer instinct or any real desire to compete.

Librans and Their Money are Soon Parted

Librans need to be high earners or they need to be married to them because they really know how to spend money. These subjects have excellent taste and an unerring eye for the best, and this makes them high maintenance marriage partners. They love eating in the nicest restaurants, belonging to the best clubs and taking vacations in glitzy hotels and locations. Despite their profligacy (or perhaps because of it), most Librans prepare for the future and they try to put money aside in pensions or savings schemes so that they won't end up short of the necessities of life.

The Libran Home

The unerring taste, refinement and style of this sign ensure that the Libran home is likely to be elegant and tasteful. Some are interested in having land and a nice garden, but all need a spacious home. They often prefer to buy a slightly run down house, which they can stamp their own individuality on and where they can amuse themselves by creating something beautiful. Librans like peace and quiet, so while they are always happy to have company and to entertain, they don't encourage people to drop in unannounced or to hang around the place using it as a free hotel. They need a room or place that they can call their own so that they can retreat, watch sports on the television, read a book and recharge their batteries.

Libra Relationships

This sign of the zodiac is supposed to be especially attuned to relationships and to looking for perfect love, but is it? I have known Librans who stay in the same relationship for years, those who move to a new lover every few years and yet others who lose out in matters of the heart and become embittered. Many are happy to live alone, with just the occasional foray out in the world. Some of them marry and then are congenitally unable to be faithful to a partner, despite the fact that they love their spouse. Some have a partner who acts as a kind of mother figure. I remember one man, who was married for many years and unfaithful throughout the marriage, telling me that, when a girlfriend left him, he didn't feel too cut up about it because he always had the wife at home to turn to and to mother him until he got over it. What does appear to be a frequent element is for Librans to feel incomplete without a partner, not necessarily that they are suited to the partnership life.

Librans love their children, but not to the point where they sacrifice too much of their own freedom or put themselves last. There is a slight coldness attached to this sign that detaches them from others in some strange way. Some have a strong sex-drive, sexual curiosity and need for excitement gets them into scrapes but some don't have any real feelings. Some are extremely argumentative and critical, but others are kindness itself.

Health

Librans are either sick to the point of being handicapped or as strong as horses. Some make a fuss when they are ill; others just get on with it. The weak spots are the kidneys, bladder and pancreas, which means that some suffer from things like cystitis, kidney problems or diabetes, which in turn can lead to kidney failure. Some have chronic spinal or nerve damage, which affects their walking.

A Few Stray Facts

Librans enjoy being members of sports clubs, but they prefer the social aspects of these rather than the sports themselves. They do love to dance though, so this is probably their best form of exercise.

Librans love listening to music, and some play an instrument.

Male Librans love to discuss abstract facts and to talk about ideas; they find conversations about feelings and personal lives boring, though females are happy to discuss personal matters as well as abstracts.

All the Librans I have come across are good self-taught cooks and most can decorate a home with ease.

Librans have a graceful and neat way of carrying themselves and they always try to look good.

Libra Decans

The first Decan is also Libra, but the second is Aquarius and the third Gemini. Read through the brief descriptions below and then turn to the chapters on Aquarius and Gemini.

1st Decan, Libra

Pure Libra. This adds to all the classic Libran characteristics of intelligence and a sense of justice. These subjects see every side of an argument, which can make it hard for them to come to a decision. They need their surroundings at work and at home to be clean, tidy and attractive. Sometimes, shoveling papers and muddle out of sight into cupboards, so that they can't find them when they need to! Relationships and friendships are extremely important to them, but they are quite happy to compartmentalize them. There is a sharp intuition, allowing these people to sum up others instantly.

2nd Decan, Aquarius

There is a slightly offbeat side to these Librans, because the Aquarian influence adds a touch of eccentricity and originality. It also adds a strong sense of justice and an idealistic attitude that is sometimes out of touch with reality. This influence brings a wonderful sense of humor, deep intelligence and wisdom, but it can lead to a lack of common sense. These subjects are more steadfast in relationships than the other two, and while they can happily live alone, they prefer to have a partner.

3rd Decan, Gemini

This adds humor and a very quick mind, which is more businesslike than either of the other two Decan types. There is far more attachment to partnerships in this case, and if one goes wrong, this Libran won't find it as easy to walk away and forget about it as the other two types can. The Gemini influence can add restlessness, a desire for job variety, or a changeable work history. These people are the best communicators of the three Decan types. These subjects may suffer from lower spine problems that affects their legs.

Libra Dwaads

The first Dwaad is also Libra, so no change here. For all other Dwaads, read the chapter on the sign in question and also the brief descriptions below to see what adjustments are made to the original sign.

Sign	What is added
Libra	Pure Libra.
Scorpio	Deeper feelings, deep thought, intuition and talent for investigation.
Sagittarius	A sense of humor, a desire for the good life, idealism, spirituality.
Capricorn	Business sense, better control of money, dry sense of humor, verbosity.
Aquarius	Originality, eccentricity, good communication skills, unrealistic attitude.
Pisces	A mystical streak, interest in the arts and music, need for personal space.
Aries	Go-ahead attitude, tough-mindedness, leadership qualities.
Taurus	Artistic talent, love of music, creativity. Could be self-indulgent.
Gemini	Nervousness, intelligence, intellectual curiosity, friendliness.
Cancer	Love of home and family, business ability, caution in money matters.
Leo	Love of luxury, sense of grandeur, generosity, love of family.
Virgo	Intellect, ability to think deeply, interest in offbeat subjects.

Sun Sign Scorpio

October 23 to November 21
Ruling planet: Pluto (ancient ruler: Mars)
Symbol: The Scorpion
Gender: Feminine
Feminine sign types are introverts who are more thorough and patient than the masculine sign types. These types can put up with quite a lot of hardship.

The Water Group

Cancer, Scorpio, Pisces

Water sign people respond slowly when asked a question and they turn round slowly when called. These people need time to grasp new ideas because they need to filter them through their feelings before they can make up their minds. Their feelings run deep and they can be very emotional. When upset, they sulk, brood and they can even be cruel towards those who are close to them. They are extremely intuitive, they sum people up accurately, and they tend to feel everything that is going on in the surrounding atmosphere. They use this knowledge to avoid falling into traps that others simply don't see. Water sign people can be attracted to the world of business where their shrewdness and good grasp of money-matters stands them in good stead. Trust is important to them and they prefer to ally themselves to those who they can trust and rely upon.

Water sign people can love very deeply, but some of them save their greatest love for their children or for animals. They keep sensitive feelings hidden, sometimes even from themselves, and this allows irritation and resentment to build up. Once this happens, they either fall into depression or explode - much to the surprise and hurt of those who are around them. Water sign people are restless and they like to get out and about with their work and their social life, they also love to travel and explore new places. Having said this, they also need a base, a secure home and an office, shop or workshop that they can call their own. Environments are important to them and too much noise or disturbance upsets them.

The Fixed Quality
Taurus, Leo, Scorpio, Aquarius

Fixed signs try to maintain the status quo, and most prefer a well-ordered life, because too much change makes them uncomfortable. Taureans, Leos and Scorpios need financial security and they fear getting into debt, although Aquarians are less concerned about this. A happy relationship and emotional security is important to these people, and they try to work out the problems within a relationship, if at all possible, rather than giving up at the first hurdle. All fixed sign people are obstinate, which may make their life and the lives of those around them difficult in some ways, but this is beneficial in other ways because when they take on a large task, they do it thoroughly and see it through to a conclusion. Fixed sign people can put up with boredom and repetition if a job requires it, but outside of work they enjoy change and novelty as much as any other type. They have a responsible attitude to life and they take their duties seriously.

Scorpio Looks

There are three totally different types of body shape and appearance for people born under this sign, all of which are typical, but each in a totally different way. The first is a very rounded body shape, topped by a rather flat face with wide eyes and a slightly inscrutable expression. The second is a very small thin body, typical of a jockey, this being topped with a sharply angular face, a large nose and a rather serious, or indeed, fierce expression. The third is a variation on the second, being about average height and slim. The features are strong and the expression is serious when the face is relaxed. If Scorpios start out slim, they stay that way throughout life, but if they start out overweight, they stay that way too. In short, Scorpios are either very good-looking indeed or really quite plain. Most Scorpios make fearless eye contact and some have a really magnetic and penetrating gaze. Most also have thick, abundant, wavy hair which needs very little attention from a hairdresser. Their habit of going strangely blank while thinking can make others write them off as being stupid - and Scorpios are far from being stupid.

Main Characteristics

Scorpios tend to be all or nothing types, and while some astrology books tell us that Scorpios are oversexed, obsessive, untrustworthy and unpredictable, the truth is that these people do have extremely strong emotions which can bubble up to the surface very quickly, but they also have kind hearts and a strong sense of justice. Many love animals and find them easier to relate to than humans, but many are also extremely loyal and loving family members. Scorpio secretiveness is famous, but those who seek to keep secrets from them need to watch out!

General Character

Scorpios act on a combination of intuition and logic, but there are times when both go out of the window and they then run on adrenaline and emotion. This can make their behavior difficult for their friends and relatives to fathom. Another problem is that their moods change quickly from elation to depression, which can be frightening for those who have to cope with them.

Often their hearts are in the right places and they don't mean to hurt, but their sharp, critical tongues can cut to the quick. Sometimes their weirdness is caused by fear of censure or mockery by others, which makes them conciliatory to bosses and those who they deal with outside the home, but apt to take their anger and resentment out on their loved ones when they get home. Scorpios often have difficult early lives and they can harbor deep resentments and grudges against those who have hurt them in the past, so they often see themselves as victims. Their early experiences can make them suspicious and mistrustful of the motives of others.

Despite the negative sides to these subjects, there are also many positive ones. They are usually extremely loyal and faithful to those who they like and trust and they can be depended upon in most situations. If a friend, relative or neighbor needs help, the Scorpio is there at once to offer it. They have an inner strength and resilience that takes them through difficult situations and their tenacity and determination mean that they usually win out in the end. They fight fiercely on behalf of those who they love or whose causes they champion. Scorpios are hard and reliable workers, but strangely they prefer a position just below the top than being in charge. They can exercise leadership when needed, but they are best off allied to someone steadier and less emotional or irrational than themselves. In such a situation, they make excellent lieutenants who can be relied on when the chips are down. When these subjects take on a project, they are organized, logical and thorough and they see it through to the end. Their courage in difficult situations is legendary, as is their tenacity and determination. These people are the strongest and the weakest of all the signs, so they need to be allied to those whose characters fill in the gaps in their own natures. Just as Scorpios remember those who have hurt them, they also remember those who have been there for them.

Scorpio Careers

Any important, vital or heavy job appeals to these active and energetic people. Many find their way into the armed forces where their courage and love of adventure stand them in good stead. Their love of the sea often takes them into the navy. The same goes for police work, where their wonderful investigative instincts and curiosity about people come to their aid. This curiosity about human nature can lead Scorpios into psychiatry or psychology. Biology and the workings of the body interest Scorpios, which takes many of them into medical work, surgery or work in the alternative health fields. Many love the drama of working as ambulance drivers, paramedics and surgeons. The attraction to sharp objects and weapons and an aptitude for handling tools of all kinds can take them into such diverse careers as hunting, butchery, engineering and dressmaking.

Money Matters

Most Scorpios are cautious when it comes to money, always keeping something back for a rainy day. Some are quite the opposite, spending their own and everybody else's money very freely, but most are hard workers who can always earn themselves out of a hole, even by moonlighting at an extra job if necessary. Scorpios hate wasting money on unnecessary items and they don't rush out to the shops in a fit of depression. When they do spend money, they do it in the same way that they do everything else; that is in style and in a grand manner. Scorpios are not noted for generosity. Some are good to their loved ones, but careful where strangers are concerned, some are simply stingy.

Scorpio Homes

Scorpios need privacy, so apartment blocks are not for them, they need to be able to separate themselves from the lives of others and to have walls that are thick enough or an area of land that is large enough to separate them from their neighbors.

They are good neighbors because they are polite, pleasant and mildly sociable. Scorpios don't intrude on others, but they can always be relied on to help out when necessary. Some are quite untidy, and this is not helped by their habit of collecting all kinds of interesting objects and books by the ton, which fill up every available space and spill over on to the rest. They can cook well, but they are not usually keen on it, so they intersperse home- made meals with all those wonderful supermarket goodies.

Scorpio Relationships

Scorpios can live alone, but this is usually less a matter of choice than of being between lovers. Scorpios need sex, but more importantly they need to express love and affection. Once they commit, they are extremely loyal and deeply loving, and they stick to a loved partner through thick and thin. Despite this, Scorpios are also extremely independent and they don't like to lean on others or to be under an obligation to them.

As parents, they are affectionate and extremely proud of their children. Some can be hard on their children or they can allow their emotional neediness to spill over from adult relationships. As long as they curb their tendency to criticize and blame others or to act the martyr, they can make the most wonderful partners, parents and friends. Deep-seated emotional problems that are left over from childhood can manifest later as resentment, possessiveness and unreasonable jealousy, and this too can destroy what might otherwise be a successful relationship.

Health

When Scorpios get sick, they do a good job of it and they do seem to go in for death defying operations, but they then surprise all those who write them off by overcoming problems and recovering well. They are extremely good patients, and even those who drive their families crazy under normal circumstances are no problem when they are sick. They don't complain and they do their best to recover and they take all the right steps. They reach age in good health until very shortly before death takes them. Scorpio weak spots are the digestion, the reproductive organs and the spine.

A Few Stray Facts

Scorpios are competitive and they like to be the best. This means that they excel in sports, education and anything else that they put their minds to.

Scorpios like to eat fruit and vegetables, but they also have a very sweet tooth.

Most Scorpios love music and they find that listening to music or playing it gives their tense and bottled up emotions an instant outlet. However, their sensitive hearing makes them discriminating about the type of music they enjoy. Also, they don't appreciate loud noises such as the road being dug up close to where they live or work.

Scorpios are either truly wonderful, loving and kind, or utterly cruel and selfish.

The Scorpio motto is: if you are going to do something, do it properly.

Scorpio Decans

The first Decan is always Scorpio, but the second is Pisces and the third is Cancer. Read through the brief descriptions below, and then turn to the chapters on Pisces and Cancer.

1st Decan, Scorpio

Pure Scorpio. All the extremes outlined above apply, so these subjects need to guard against shooting themselves in the foot by allowing their feelings to dominate them, either at work or in personal relationships. On the other hand, their reliability, loyalty, loving heart and honesty can make them the best of the best. Scorpio emotions run high and the feelings are deep, but there is a touch of cruelty here, which others don't always appreciate.

2nd Decan, Pisces

The Piscean influence adds a touch of mysticism to the natural intuition of this sign, which leads many of them into psychic work or some form of alternative medicine. These Scorpios love to travel and they can be very independent, but at the same time surprisingly demanding of the time and attention of others. Scorpios of this Decan are less money minded than the other Scorpio types.

3rd Decan, Cancer

These Scorpios are far more home loving and family minded than either of the other two types. They love to travel and they enjoy novelty. These Scorpios can do well in a small business of their own, although they also make reliable and capable employees. These Scorpios understand money and business and they can be quite successful, but they can also be moody, sarcastic and possessive.

Scorpio Dwaads

The first Dwaad is Scorpio, so no change here. For all other Dwaads, read the chapter on the sign in question and also the brief descriptions given below to see what adjustments are made to the original sign.

Sign	What is added
Scorpio	Pure Scorpio.
Sagittarius	Independence and a need to get around from place to place.
Capricorn	Good business sense, seriousness, coping ability, hidden emotions.
Aquarius	A touch of eccentricity, obstinacy, loyalty, a lack of reality.
Pisces	Intuition, compassion, love of animals, travel and mysticism.
Aries	Courage, competitiveness, assertiveness, team spirit, less resentment.
Taurus	Love of music, artistry, talent for building, craftwork, cooking etc.
Gemini	Like the Scarlet Pimpernel, now you see him, now you don't!
Cancer	Intuition, moodiness, need for a stable home, love of travel.
Leo	High standards, tendency to hold grudges and to dramatize things.
Virgo	Interest in health matters, well-organized worker, intellect.
Libra	Artistry, love of music, less fraught nature but can be unrealistic.

Sun Sign Sagittarius

November 22 to December 21
Ruling planet: Jupiter
Symbol: The Archer, sometimes the Centaur
Gender: Masculine
This indicates an extrovert, active, courageous and somewhat pushy nature.

The Element of Fire

Aries, Leo, Sagittarius

Fire sign people do things quickly and they don't allow the grass to grow under their feet. They may commit themselves to a course of action and then regret it because they haven't given themselves enough time to think things through. On the other hand, while others are procrastinating and putting off unpleasant chores or simply not getting their act together, the fire signs are well on the way to finishing the job. Fire people display initiative, courage and leadership qualities. Some are genuinely selfish; while others are so quick to think and act that they leave others behind in their haste to get on with things. Despite their apparent selfishness, many are idealists who really do want to make the world a better place.

Fire sign people have no patience with those who hesitate, and they don't understand that it is not necessarily someone else's karma to grasp every opportunity that comes along. These subjects are quick, intelligent, humorous and generous and they love their friends and family. They become angry when others oppose them and irritable when they are tired or hungry, and they can be extremely cutting when they are wound up, but they rarely sulk. They need a good standard of living to keep up with their spending habits. Fire sign people are often passionate lovers who live life to the full.

Fire sign people are less confident than they appear and they can suddenly lose faith in themselves and become depressed when too much goes wrong. They need a steady and reliable partner who will respect them for their undoubted talents and who doesn't seek to undermine them. In turn, fire sign people need to be reminded to validate their partner and not to build up their own ego at the expense of others.

Fire sign people are often very underweight as children; they soon get over this, and they can become quite heavy later in life.

The Mutable Quality
Gemini, Virgo, Sagittarius, Pisces

Mutable signs need variety and change and this may take them into careers, which ensure that each day is different from the next. Some prefer the kind of job that takes them from one place to another, while others travel far afield. Many work in one place, but deal with a variety of people or tasks during the course of each day. Mutable sign people may choose unconventional jobs or lifestyles because it is more important for their work to fit in with their beliefs or to fulfil their spiritual needs. Many work in fields that either expand people's minds, such as writing or publishing, while others work in fields that expand their experiences, such as the travel trade or psychic work. These people sometimes choose to work in jobs that improve the lot of others, even though they can't earn much or climb the ladder of material success this way. There is a streak of independence and unconventionality about all the mutable signs, although this is less obvious in Gemini and Virgo, than it is in Sagittarius and Pisces. Many mutable sign types marry when young and start their families early. However, these early relationships all too frequently break up and they may go through a period of experimentation with a variety of partners before settling down again.

Sagittarian Looks

Sagittarians come in a variety of shapes and sizes, some are tall and raw boned, others small and thin and yet others have large chests or hips. The main distinguishing feature, like the Centaur sign, is that their top halves are often different from their bottom halves, and some have large bottoms that are out of proportion to the rest of them. Their best feature is often their hair which is abundant, wavy and lustrous and often (in white races) a reddish blond color.

Main Characteristics

These people get bored if they have to stay in the same place for very long, so they often work in jobs that take them from place to place. They are often extremely clever with their hands and able to build or make anything. They have a great sense of humor and they are honest to the point of bluntness. Many think deeply and work out a belief system that means something to them and they are outraged by injustice.

General Character

Sagittarians are honest to the point of being blunt and tactless at times. They don't have time for lies or manipulation, so what you see is usually what you get. There is a childlike quality about these people, which can manifest itself in a refusal to accept commitment or they may display babyish behavior when they are off color or unhappy. This same childlike quality makes them great youth workers or teachers who are happy to be with children of any age, and this naturally also makes them wonderful parents. Sagittarians are wonderfully accepting, non-hostile and easy to get along with, although they are often nicer as friends than as close relatives or partners.

Sagittarians need freedom and they don't like being quizzed about where they have been or what they have been up to. Their honesty ensures that if they say that they have been in a certain place or with a particular group of people - that is the exact truth. Sagittarians have fine legal minds and they hate injustice, so this can take them into fields such as legal work or arbitration. These people enjoy talking and listening and they can happily spend a day debating with their friends. They are extremely sociable and great company at a party. They make good friends, but their tendency to take off to pastures new from time to time makes them somewhat unreliable. Some Sagittarians are world travelers who backpack their way to the wildest and most remote areas. Their curiosity about anything that is remote or hidden from normal view is legendary. This often leads many of them into work in astrology, clairvoyance, the paranormal and spiritual healing.

The worst Sagittarian fault is a tendency to grumble and to consider themselves hard done by, even when their lives are actually quite easy, but they are extremely kind and helpful, which lays them open to advantage takers. However, these subjects are also extremely broad-minded and they embrace or take an interest in people of all races, cultures and classes of society, because everything interests them. They are idealistic and they will fight for the rights of the underdog if they can. Most are interested in education and they will do all they can to pass on their own specialized forms of knowledge to others.

Sagittarian Careers

The most obvious career choice for any Sagittarian is teaching, and especially teaching children and young people, where their infectious sense of fun can make learning enjoyable. Their affinity with words and sense of justice can take them into the legal field and in this arena, their sociability and "club-able" nature also stands them in good stead. Many find full or part-time work in astrology or the spiritual fields of work, and even those who are not involved are very often open to offbeat or alternative ideas.

Sagittarians are good with their hands, so when this is allied to their preference for peripatetic jobs takes many of them into the fields of carpentry, electrical work, building, plumbing, plastering, laying paths and so on. They are not particularly good at paperwork or figure work, so a spouse or business partner often ends up handling this for them. Others work as free-lance editors, broadcasters or writers, which taps into their affinity with words and their need for variety, fun and freedom.

Most don't do very well at school, possibly because they find the group atmosphere and the need to accept the beliefs and opinions of others far too restricting. However, most return to study in some form or other later in life. Some take up music, sport or some other interest that becomes a career later on. Often these subjects are more attuned to the land than to office work or city life, and they enjoy working with or for the benefit of animals.

Some Sagittarians are drawn to show business and their sense of humor often takes them into the field of comedy, indeed many of the world's top comedians come from this sign. Others are real showmen, perhaps tapping into an unusual talent and making it pay. Sports are another major arena for this sign because they are often naturals at whatever sport they decide to take up. They have enough competitive spirit to make a success of their game, but they can easily destroy their careers by strange behavior, drunkenness and a lack of self-discipline. These subjects are best when they are striving to reach the top than when they actually get there. This is the sign of the traveler and to them; it is better to travel than to arrive.

Sagittarians love to travel and to meet a variety of people. Tradition says that Sagittarians love horses and everything about the people and atmosphere of the horse world. Many love to gamble, so the world of racing suits them very well. Others are attracted to sport or to show-business. Either way, the motivation is to do something that is out of the ordinary.

Money and Sagittarius

Sagittarians are not money minded. Their values are spiritual rather than material. Some can be successful in their work, but many just do what they can to make a living and leave it at that. Many Sagittarians achieve success in sport or show business, and this brings in a great deal of money. In this case, the first thing they do with it is to help their families out, keeping a little back for themselves for a rainy day. They need a secure base even if their job takes them traveling, so they will save for a home and also to educate their children.

Home is Where the Suitcases are Kept

Sagittarians may get around with their jobs but they need a nice home to come back to. Many love the countryside or the sea, so given the chance they will live out of town rather than in the center of things. They also need somewhere to keep their vehicles, as they often have more than one. These subjects vary between being extremely tidy or totally uncaring about their homes so there is no standard style of housework. Most can cook very well when they are in the mood to do so and they do like to eat well.

Sagittarian Relationships

Once again, it is hard to categorize these subjects. Some are real relaters whose homes are filled with relatives, friends and pets, while others need to be free to roam the world. Either way, they need to be able to take off in a fishing boat or to visit friends in other parts of the country if the mood takes them. Even when marriage was the norm Sagittarians often preferred to remain single, and some can jump from one partner to another at will. Others need the security of a normal relationship, while others are perfectly happy with their own company in addition to a few friends dropping in every now and again. If they want to meet a new partner, their cheerful, humorous and friendly manner ensures that this is easy for them. They can be extremely cutting, sarcastic and even domineering and dictatorial at times, and their occasional bouts of argumentative nature and unpleasantness can be the cause of marriage breakdowns. Some find it very hard to show affection, and they forget to be romantic or to do those little things that show their partner that they are loved. These people prefer to do something practical for their partner, such as making a nice meal or putting up shelves.

Sagittarians can go through periods of total celibacy, but when they are in the mood for sex, their drive is quite high. Some find it hard to commit to others and they can be quite promiscuous, others will make a relationship and then be unfaithful when the mood takes them. Yet others are perfectly faithful. There are no set rules where this sign is concerned. When they do decide to explore, there are no boundaries; they will try anything that is new and different.

Health

Sagittarians worry about their health and their conversation often revolves around this. They do suffer from a variety of irritating ailments, but they still manage to live full and fruitful lives. Their traditional weak spots are the hips and thighs, but many have digestive problems possibly as a result of stress. Some Sagittarians develop mental problems after a period of intense stress.

A Few Stray Facts

Many Sagittarians grow up in a religious atmosphere, often among people who have particularly rigid beliefs. They then question this and look around for something more meaningful to themselves.

Sagittarians often find luck, love and work in a country other than that which they were born in. Alternatively, their parents are immigrants, which means that they grow up with two cultures and at least two languages. These people love to travel and to meet people from different backgrounds to themselves. They are curious about other lifestyles, religions and outlooks and they don't have preconceived notions about people of a different race, religion, culture or standard of living. Everything interests them.

Sagittarians can be far more eccentric than even the wildest of any of the other signs.

Sagittarian Decans

The first Decan is also Sagittarius, but the second is Aries and the third is Leo. Read through the brief descriptions below and then turn to the chapters on Aries and Leo.

1st Decan, Sagittarius

The pure Sagittarian spirit of honesty, love of freedom and the tendency to question accepted rules, which are laid down by others, is at its strongest here. These people march to their own drumbeat and search for their own destiny, wherever it takes them. They will either settle into teaching, religious, philosophical or legal work or take off and make a life and a career out of something that is truly different.

2nd Decan, Aries

The Aries influence introduces competitiveness and a talent for sports and games, so this is where the sportsmen and women tend to be found. This adds courage but also a tendency to argue or even to bully others when the opportunity arises. However, the idealism of Aries often takes the Sagittarian into humanitarian work or something that improves the planet. Many of these are excellent craftsmen and women or engineers.

3rd Decan, Leo

The Leo love of drama and of being center stage can lead to a career in show business, sport or the media. This type wants to live on a grand scale and the normal mundane existence of ordinary people bores them. Sometimes this need for drama is played out in the wider world as a career, at other times it leads the Sagittarian to explore philosophy, spirituality and astrology, so that even if their way of life is fairly normal, their inner world is exciting.

Sagittarian Dwaads

The first Dwaad is also Sagittarius, so no change here. For all other Dwaads, read the chapter on the sign in question and also the brief descriptions given below to see what adjustments are made to the original sign.

Sign	What is added
Sagittarius	Pure Sagittarius.
Capricorn	Adds practicality, business sense, materialism and ambition.
Aquarius	Adds originality and eccentricity to an already eccentric personality.
Pisces	The true mystic who makes spirituality or religion a way of life.
Aries	An outgoing nature with a great sense of humor and a love of sports.
Taurus	Adds creativity and a real talent for building, gardening or farming.
Gemini	Adds sociability, intelligence, curiosity, but also nervousness.
Cancer	Oddly enough, this adds acting ability and interest in media work.
Leo	Adds the love of drama, generosity, talent and organizational talents.
Virgo	Intellect, academic interests and an ability to handle details.
Libra	Can make the Sagittarian lazy or apt to lean on others.
Scorpio	This combination adds intuition and an interest in occult matters.

Sun Sign Capricorn

December 22 to January 19
Ruling planet: Saturn
Symbol: The Goat
Gender: Feminine
Feminine sign types are introverts who are more thorough and
patient than the masculine sign types. These types can put up
with quite a lot of hardship.

The Element of Earth
Taurus, Virgo, Capricorn

These are practical, diligent and hard working people who are happiest when they are doing something useful. They can be relied upon, and even though it might take them a while to get around to things but they usually get there in the end. These people are more ambitious than they appear and they may be shrewd operators in politics or in business. Their drawbacks are sometimes a lack of speed when action is needed, stubbornness, greed and distaste for chancy ventures or of spending money unnecessarily.

Most earth sign people are family types who need the security of a good relationship. They rarely walk away from family responsibility, even when one or two family members are difficult to cope with. These subjects are sensual and loving, especially in a relationship that is comfortable and that gives them confidence. They may have a creative streak, although this manifests itself in different ways for each sign. Shrewd and cautious, they need material and emotional security and they can put up with a lot in order to get it. Many earth types appear tight-fisted, they can be shortsighted about financial matters and this is often due to a real or imagined fear of poverty.

The Cardinal Quality
Aries, Cancer, Libra, Capricorn
Cardinal types don't let the grass grow under their feet and they are inclined to do what they think is best for themselves, their family or their group. They can put themselves out to fit in with others, where necessary, but they can't leave their own needs too far out in the cold. When the chips are down they know that they can depend upon themselves. Once they have made their minds up (and this includes the vacillating sign of Libra), they can't be pushed from their path. Cardinal people usually take advantage of opportunities, they make the most of them and they can be good leaders as long as they allow others an opinion and an opportunity to use their creativity. One thing they are often good at is motivating and encouraging others, but they may then ask or expect too much of others. Despite the strength of this type, their confidence can evaporate and they need the support of a partner or at the very least a couple of good friends.

Capricorn Looks
Capricorns tend to look old when young, but they make up for this in later life because they don't seem to change very much as time goes by. These subjects are usually around average or slightly less than average height. Some are fairly plump throughout life, and if so, they have a larger top half than bottom half. Those who start out slim, remain that way which can make them bony and gawky when young but stunning when they get older. Capricorn faces have strong features and good bones, which also helps their looks in later life. Some have wonderful hair, which they often wear quite long; others have fine hair that clings to their small neat heads.

Main Characteristics

Capricorns are ambitious, and if they don't have much in the way of personal ambition, they push their loved ones and their children to succeed. These people are family minded and they can't cope if a relationship breaks up, often because they rely upon their spouse to give their self-confidence a boost. Capricorns are highly intelligent and extremely sensitive. They sometimes hide their light under a bushel.

General Character

Capricorns seem to come in fairly distinct types. Some are quiet, shy, retiring and lacking in social skills and self-confidence. These start out as gentle, watchful children who keep their heads down at school, avoid the bullies, confide in nobody and work their way up and out of whatever circumstances surround them. A difficult start in life makes these Capricorns strive to overcome the handicaps of an introverted personality and an unprepossessing family background, but they do as well as possible under the whatever circumstances they find themselves in. These studious subjects usually choose a profession where they can progress slowly upwards in and a soul mate to share their lives with.

The second Capricorn types are so outgoing that it is hard to believe that they belong to this sign at all. These subjects can be talking machines who are quite exhausting to be with. They have an impressive aura of competence and business success, which doesn't always live up to expectations, although they usually keep on trying. The success that they appear to achieve in the wider world is not always reflected in their personal lives, where their over-sensitivity can be a problem for them and for those around them. Fortunately, there is a third type, which is much more reasonable. These Capricorns are just as ambitious as the other two, but within far more normal boundaries, and their manner and behavior is more easygoing.

Whatever the outer package, Capricorns tend to tread two diametrically opposed paths at the same time. They feel a huge sense of responsibility towards their families, especially their parents, and they are dutiful towards in-laws, step or half relatives and others who they feel they must rub along with. However, they have a huge inner independence that takes them on paths that don't necessarily meet with the approval of those who are around them, or indeed of the world they inhabit. One such example is an acquaintance of mine who came from a family of upper-middle class achievers, who rejected their values in order to become a herbalist, aromatherapist and clairvoyant. Needless to say, being a Capricorn, she made a good job of this and is now the head of various societies in her fields of work.

Capricorns are often old when young and young when old. They retain their looks well into old age, and with luck they eventually grow out of whatever held them back as youngsters and lead far happier second halves to their lives than they did during the first. The main thing to bear in mind is that these people never give up. Whatever setbacks life hands them, they dust themselves off and start again and they usually end up making good in the long run. Whether introverted or apparently outgoing, Capricorns tend to keep their problems to themselves or only share them with a trusted family member. They don't wear their hearts on their sleeves.

Some are far too serious and even dour; others become far too materialistic, while some seem unable to understand that the needs and feelings of others count for anything. Some of these subjects eventually learn to trust others and to love someone other than their parents, but others never really do so.

The Serious Business of the Capricorn Career

The astrology of the twentieth century tells us that Capricorns are drawn to banking and to big business, while the astrology of earlier eras tells us that this is the sign of the scientist. The fact is that Capricorns are extremely practical, they can handle details and they can keep an amazing amount of minutiae in their heads. This does take many of them into accountancy or publishing with its emphasis on getting the details right. These subjects will obtain as good an education as they can and then fill in any gaps by attending evening classes. Typical Capricorns start out by taking a fairly lowly position in a large organization and steadily work their way up. Restructuring seems to wash over them and they eventually reach quite high positions.

Some Capricorns pick up on the energies of the eccentric signs of Sagittarius and Aquarius that border their own sign, and find themselves drawn to religion or spirituality, and there are a surprising number in the mind, body and spirit fields. Even here, their innate business sense leads them to make more of a success out of this than others who do the same thing. It seems that their practicality, tenacity, organizational ability and their habit of working hard when others skive, makes them ultimately successful in anything that they decide to take on. Some are serious, silent and dour, clerkish types who don't make an impression. Others are extremely outgoing folk who gravitate to sales or even to the world of show business. Most find a skill, a technique or perhaps some kind of medical job like dentistry, chiropody, working in a vet's or a pharmacy and stick with this. They perfect their skills and make a living using them.

Oddly enough, some Capricorns opt for a career in show business, and once again it is their professionalism that makes them successful. Some love to sing, play music, compose music or dance.

Money and Capricorns Are Not Easily Parted

Capricorns have much common sense and practicality where money is concerned. They often go through fairly lengthy periods of low income and hard times before they reach the level where their income improves. They rarely grumble, but manage on what they have and still put a little aside for a rainy day, and when the money starts coming in they put a good deal of it aside. These hard workers will always find a way of earning themselves and their families out of trouble if the need arises. They fear poverty and this can make them unnecessarily tight-fisted.

Home Life

Oddly enough for such a sensible and materialistic sign (and despite their natural tendency to save and invest), they don't always buy property, possibly due to a peculiar need for these subjects to keep their options open. This can take them into renting property, or even taking space in homes that belong to other people. Some Capricorns are late developers who stay at home with their parents until they themselves are middle aged. Indeed, some never leave and only become property owners once their parents die. When they buy a home, they keep it in reasonable order and they buy whatever is needed for reasonable comfort. They don't necessarily feel the need to up-date or improve on things that still have some years of life left in them, but when they do buy something they don't buy flashy gimmicky stuff but things that will last. The one thing that Capricorns don't stint on is warmth. Despite the chilly nature of some Capricorns, they cannot stand being cold, so their homes are far from chilly. They tend to be good cooks, so neither they nor their families are likely to go short of a good meal or two.

Capricorn Relationships

This is a total win or lose situation for Capricorns, and there are many scenarios in which they can find themselves. Some are so attached to their parents that they never really venture out into the world of love and marriage, or they only feel free to do so when their parents have gone and they themselves are getting old. Others go to the other extreme and marry when very young with varying rates of success. Those who are lucky enough to get it right are the most loyal and loving of partners, who would never dream of straying from the marital nest. If they are lucky enough to find the right partner, they eventually relax, blossom and learn to do things that please them, to socialize and to enjoy life.

Some Capricorns are far too controlling or fussy, and they can take offence over every little thing. This doesn't make it easy for others to stay in love with them or even to want to hang around for very long. Others are perfectly reasonable and happy to be part of the rough and tumble of family life. Yet others form immensely strong attachments to their partners and to their children and they strive to make everyone around them as happy as possible. As I said at the start, it is either win or lose in the partnership stakes. They certainly love their children, but may they work so much that they miss out on the fun aspects of parenting.

Health

Some Capricorns are quite sick when young, but they eventually grow out of whatever ails them and go on to live healthy lives. Indeed, they belong to the longest-lived of all the Sun signs. The weak spots are the skin and bones. Many are hard of hearing and nowadays some have operations to clear up weaknesses in the inner ear. Some suffer from asthma or eczema in childhood, but they manage to live with or overcome these setbacks later in life.

A Few Stray Facts

This is the least athletic sign of the zodiac, but many Capricorns take up some form of sport or game later in life. I know one who took swimming lessons in his fifties, and another who took up golf upon retirement. Some enjoy singing or dancing.

Capricorns don't wear their feelings on their sleeves, so it can be hard to know where one stands with them.

These subjects can be wonderful with animals, and they sometimes find them easier to love than humans.

Capricorns are best left to do things in their own time. They get through everything that they need to do, but they become agitated and lose track of themselves if they are rushed.

These people can be shortsighted over money matters, and in some cases they can even be surprisingly crooked, especially when ambition or the need to hang on to power gets into their bloodstream. Remember Capricorn tricky-dicky President Nixon!

If they are encouraged to relax and enjoy life, they love to travel. They tend to opt for cruises where they can see many different places, but do the actual moving from place to place in comfort.

Capricorn Decans

The first Decan is also Capricorn, but the second is Taurus and the third is Virgo. Read through the brief descriptions below and then turn to the chapters on Taurus and Virgo.

1st Decan, Capricorn

Pure Capricorn. These subjects are either very outgoing or very shy. They are highly intelligent, very sensitive and sometimes apt to push others away in an effort to avoid being hurt. They are sensible, thorough, capable and hard working and they can also be surprisingly ambitious. When they give their hearts they are extremely loyal and they appreciate loyalty in others. These Capricorns are studious and serious.

2nd Decan, Taurus

This is probably the easiest of all the Decans, as the Taurean influence adds sociability, creativity, a touch of artistry and makes for a more relaxed and easier-going personality. These people can make a nice home and create a lovely garden, because they enjoy large projects of this kind. This influence brings pleasure from music and often a good sense of rhythm and a love of dancing.

3rd Decan, Virgo

These Capricorns are highly intelligent and they can be extremely studious. They are likely to become experts in their chosen fields. Their lack of self-confidence can hold them back when they are young, but they grow into themselves and become more comfortable to be with as they get older. These subjects must guard against miserliness and fussiness.

Capricorn Dwaads

The first Dwaad is also Capricorn, so no change here. For all other Dwaads, read the chapter on the sign in question and also the brief descriptions given below to see what adjustments are made to the original sign.

Sign	What is added
Capricorn	Pure Capricorn.
Aquarius	A touch of eccentricity, a scientific mind and some offbeat interests.
Pisces	An interest in unusual subjects, sensitivity, emotional vulnerability.
Aries	This is a real self-starter who needs to get to the top to be happy.
Taurus	Artistic or creative talent, expressed in a practical way. Thoroughness.
Gemini	Adds nervousness and fussiness, but also sociability and wide interests.
Cancer	This is a real homemaker and family person who also loves animals.
Leo	Adds a touch of extraversion, affection and an ability to enjoy life.
Virgo	This brings intelligence, concentration on details and financial acumen.
Libra	Adds sociability, artistry, determination, and a desire for partnerships.
Scorpio	Some resentment over early difficulties, also intuition and sexuality.
Sagittarius	A sense of humor, a need for fun and an interest in travel.

Sun Sign Aquarius

January 20 to February 18
Ruling planet: Uranus (ancient ruler: Saturn)
Symbol: The Water Carrier
Gender: Masculine
This indicates an extrovert, active, courageous and somewhat
pushy nature.

The Element of Air
Gemini, Libra, Aquarius

The air sign mind is always active. Whether they are humming tunes in their head or playing out ideas and daydreams, their brains are rarely still. Many of them are sociable and friendly and their homes may be filled with neighbors, friends and relatives who pop in or stay for a night or two. Many are good at crafts, handiwork and mechanical tasks, and most seem to be able to cope very well with household tasks such as decorating or do-it-themselves jobs. Some love to collect tools, equipment or gadgets. They come up with wonderfully inventive answers to other people's problems, although they can find it hard to solve their own. They are excellent communicators and they may spend hours on the phone or the computer. They can be restless and tenser than they appear and they need a mildly sporting outlet or a change of scene on occasion to help them keep a healthy balance. Many are excellent teachers.

Air sign people are sympathetic to the plight of others, but they aren't good at shouldering the burdens of others for too long as this wears down their own delicate nervous systems. They may seek to protect their sensitive nerves by behaving in a way that is critical or unfeeling towards those who are close to them. Most air sign people are hopeless with those who are sick and they may lack patience with family members who become ill or downhearted. Air sign people can touch with reality, either by worrying about things that are not important or by living in a kind of fantasy-land.

The Fixed Quality
Taurus, Leo, Scorpio, Aquarius
Fixed people try to maintain the status quo, and most prefer a well-ordered life, because too much change makes them uncomfortable. Taureans, Leos and Scorpios need financial security and they fear getting into debt, but Aquarians are less concerned about this. A happy relationship and emotional security is important to these people, and they try to work out the problems within a relationship, if at all possible, rather than giving up at the first hurdle. All fixed sign people are obstinate, which may make their life and the lives of those around them difficult in some ways but this trait becomes a benefit when they take on a large task, they do it thoroughly and see it through to a conclusion. Fixed sign people can put up with boredom and repetition if a job requires it, but outside of work they enjoy change and novelty as much as any other type. They have a responsible attitude to life and they take their duties seriously.

Aquarian Looks
Aquarians fall into two distinct categories. The lucky ones are tall, angular and very slim, and they stay that way, with perhaps a little thickening around the waist, throughout life. These Aquarians have long faces with rather prominent noses. In white races, their eyes can be very blue or very pale gray, and their gaze is very direct and somewhat magnetic. Males tend to lose their hair from a

receding hairline rather than from a spreading bald spot and both sexes can have very fine hair that is hard to manage. The second Aquarian type is short and very rounded indeed. These subjects have flat, fairly expressionless faces and they are usually blessed with much nicer hair than the other type.

Main Characteristics

Each Aquarian is a one-off, and they are so individual that they are not even like their brother Aquarians, let alone anyone else. There are quiet Aquarians and noisy ones, nice ones and nasty ones, but they are all intelligent and studious. This sign is noted for eccentricity and for original thinkers and the one archetype that does seem to fit most is that of the absentminded professor.

General Character

Aquarians either love or loathe astrology. One friend of mine, who wasn't the slightest bit interested in the subject, once told me that both he and his wife were Aquarians, that seven other members of their family were Aquarians, and that none of them were the least bit like any of the others. This, he assured me, was a sure sign that there is absolutely nothing in Sun sign astrology. Well, to start with, having a high number of one Sun sign in a family is a pretty typical astrological factor. In my own small family, we have seven Leos and six Scorpios, and those that do not belong to these signs have them rising or strongly marked on their birth charts. The other factor in favor of astrology is that nine Aquarians in one family will all be different from each other, because Aquarians are - well - different; even from each other!

These highly intelligent people don't think the way that others do. They cannot behave like sheep, or believe in what they are told to, and they have extremely strong opinions of their own. It is good that most Aquarians are humanitarian and are keen to do good things, because if this were not the case, these powerful people could become tyrants. Some are extremely eccentric folk who dress in weird clothes and who refuse to live even in a semi-normal manner, others are only marginally eccentric. One Aquarian friend of ours worked as an executive in a traditional and very normal job, but nobody in his place of work could have suspected that he was also deeply into Scientology. Traditional religion rarely interests Aquarians, so joining cults or looking into unusual beliefs and ideas comes naturally to them. Once they have thoroughly investigated whatever it was that caught their attention, if it doesn't give them the answers that they want, they drop their interest and move on to something else. Even those who do appear to be involved in a "normal" religion have often taken this up later in life, due to something in it that catches their imagination.

Aquarians collect books, magazines, papers and publications of all kinds. They need to keep up-to-date, and they like to know the ins and outs of everything that goes on in the world. They are often extremely knowledgeable, and they love to pass their knowledge on to others, which takes many of them into the realms of teaching. Most Aquarians will take up a cause of some kind at some point in their lives, sometimes to the point of obsession. Some are capable of holding down a job and making a good living, but others simply drift around, doing whatever pays the immediate bills and then moving on to something else. Aquarians are proud, but they don't need money to prove themselves successful.

Aquarian dreams are sky-high, but their grip on reality can be missing. Such things as arriving anywhere on time and coping with daily chores are often painfully difficult for them, partly because there is always something they need to do at the last minute. Some get trapped into a kind of tunnel vision that doesn't allow them to think in anything other than black and white, others can think round corners.

These people talk and move very slowly, which belies the speed and inventiveness of their brains. They appear relaxed and laid-back, but they are actually quite easily unsettled, tense and irritable - and when really rattled, they can be extremely cutting and hurtful. Oddly enough, some these subjects can suffer badly from envy or even outright jealousy, because they see others who are less intelligent, hardworking, honest, talented or deserving overtaking them in their own fields and often being far better thought of by those who employ them. Other Aquarians have all the same instincts but allied to real a talent for politics - both in the idealistic sense and also the sense of being able to worm their way up through an organization and get ahead of the competition - and these can end up as Presidents of their countries.

Aquarian Careers - or Doing Something Interesting

Aquarians are inventive and creative, so they gravitate to jobs that give them the opportunity to express this side of themselves, and they often end up running their own small businesses or being self-employed. A friend of mine once had to employ a dozen workmen to refit an office block, and eleven of the men who were commissioned to work on the project were self-employed Aquarians. The variation of personalities in this sign means that some will find work in large organizations, especially where there is an opportunity to use computers and to manipulate or design systems for them. Teaching attracts many Aquarians, as does charity work or anything offbeat, such as astrology, putting on events or simply finding a career in whatever interests them. Some prefer being on committees and saving the planet to work as such, because what they do must have real meaning to them.

When computers were a novelty, the first to obtain them were the Aquarians, and even now there can hardly be an Aquarian home that doesn't have at least one knocking around. Another career option is that of outlaw! I once read a cat burglar's autobiography, and he said that he and every one of his criminal friends were Aquarians!

Money - What Money?

Some Aquarians make money, most don't. Even if they do, they don't necessarily hang on to it. Aquarian values are spiritual rather than materialistic, and they are more interested in feeling personally fulfilled and doing something they like than in accumulating money. Some are extremely generous, others are tight-fisted; some spend money on themselves, others spend it on other people. Some collect antiques and others collect objects d'art. Most collect books, papers, computer equipment, gadgets and junk. Some seem to collect animals and relatives as well. Some are self-supporting, others are happy to drift along or to live off more organized relatives. Some have savings: most have an overdraft. If they do manage to get their act together, it is by buying a property and paying off a mortgage.

Home - or the Art of Feng "Phooey"

I had one Aquarian friend whose home was so clean, tidy and spare that a surgeon wouldn't have hesitated to operate in it, but I have another friend who lived in something that looked like a scrap-yard. Parkinson's law tells us that as soon as a space is created it will be filled, but Aquarians don't wait for Parkinson, they fill everything to overflowing before the space arises. Some regularly spend money on clothes while others rarely do so but neither type gets rid of anything, so their wardrobes are usually crammed. When they do decide to have a clear out, they take unwanted stuff to the charity or thrift shop because they can't bear to throw something away that could be made use of by others. Some have a nicely appointed and decorated home, others just don't seem to notice that the place is falling down around them. Some are great cooks; others don't even know how to use peel a potato or boil an egg.

Relationships

Aquarians live in traditional marriages, in open relationships, in communes and alone. Their arrangements can be set or fluid. Those who are more traditional may or may not have children. There is no standard arrangement. Those who do have children are very keen that their offspring should have as much education and intellectual stimulation as possible, and they also enroll their children in for every extracurricular activity they can think of. It is an odd thing, but many Aquarians bring up children who have sicknesses or handicaps, and they manage to deal with this in a cooler and more successful manner than those who are, on the face of it, more attuned to parenting.

Many Aquarians are animal lovers who cannot live without a few pets and some run a kind of hobby farm with a motley collection of animals. Others rescue animals and look after them. Some can't bear pets or animals.

Health

Aquarians can suffer from chronic ailments such as asthma, eczema, diabetes and arthritis, but they manage these ailments quite well, often turning to alternative therapies and finding something that suits them. Many are vegetarians. Many are heavy smokers, while others are virulently against smoking. Few are real drinkers, although most enjoy a drink on social occasions.

A Few Stray Facts

As you can see, this is an all-or-nothing sign, which seems to go one way or another. Some want children, others don't - and many have them, but lose touch with them after divorce and so on.

The only Aquarian similarities that I can state categorically are that all love intelligent conversation, gossip, exploring abstract ideas and having a laugh with friends. All read a lot and collect books. Most love music and collect CDs and so on. Many are into photography and have boxes of photographs in their attics.

Unless born in the Libra Decan, Aquarians are not great eaters, and this helps the slender type to remain slim throughout life. Some can happily live on coffee, cigarettes and vitamin pills.

These people are often fascinated by psychic matters, water divining, ghost busting and so on, and they attach themselves to psychic people. However they themselves are more attuned to factual, logical divinations, such as astrology and numerology.

Many Aquarians are musical and they love the theatre, but they are more likely to put on events, work the lights and set the scenery than to take center stage.

One trait that does seem to be fairly common is that of fostering talent in others. I once asked an Aquarian friend why this is so, and she told me that she hated to see intellect and ability being wasted or not being given a chance. The hatred of waste does seem to be an Aquarian theme, which is perhaps why my Aquarian husband tries to recycle everything and rarely throws anything away!

Aquarius Decans

The first Decan is also Aquarius, but the second is Gemini and the third is Libra. Read through the brief descriptions below and then turn to the chapters on Gemini and Libra.

1st Decan, Aquarius

Pure Aquarius. Apart from the intelligence, originality, inventiveness, interesting conversation and collections of books, these people are unlikely to be like anyone else on earth, including all other Aquarians. These people can be quite businesslike or very eccentric.

2nd Decan, Gemini

These Aquarian have a more flexible attitude and fewer fixed opinions than the other two types. They need variety and a change of scene and they choose careers that take them from place to place. These Aquarians enjoy family life and they need more emotional stability than other types. They are more likely to be interested in a career than the other two types, and many are interested in teaching, working with words or music.

3rd Decan, Libra

The Libran influence makes these Aquarians less tense and more easygoing. These Aquarians are more conventional than the other Decans, and they are keener on relationships and a home life. These Aquarians can be somewhat self-indulgent, but also far more artistic than the other types and more into practical things such as gardening, cooking or do-it-yourself jobs.

Aquarius Dwaads

The first Dwaad is also Aquarius, so no change here. For all other Dwaads, real the chapter on the sign in question and also the brief descriptions given below to see what adjustments are made to the original sign.

Sign	What is added
Aquarius	Pure Aquarius.
Pisces	Kindness, vulnerability, artistry. Also chaotic finances or lifestyle.
Aries	Authority, courage, enterprise, a talent for politics. Lack of realism.
Taurus	Artistry, common sense, thoroughness, fondness for family life.
Gemini	Intelligence, speed of thought and action, interest in words and teaching.
Cancer	Love of home and family, fondness for animals, caution.
Leo	Humor, generosity, love of family, children and the limelight.
Virgo	Aptitude for details, care and caution, common sense and practicality.
Libra	Artistry, flirtatiousness, talent. May be totally unrealistic.
Scorpio	Intuition, caution, common sense, thoroughness, acumen.
Sagittarius	So far out with the fairies that they never come back down to earth.
Capricorn	Common sense, aptitude for computers and figures, fondness for parents.

Sun Sign Pisces

February 19 to March 20
Ruling planet: Neptune (ancient ruler: Jupiter)
Symbol: The Fish
Gender: Feminine
Feminine sign types are introverts who are more thorough and patient than the masculine sign types. These types can put up with quite a lot of hardship.

The Water Group
Cancer, Scorpio, Pisces

Water sign people respond slowly when asked a question and they turn round slowly when called. These people need time to grasp new ideas because they need to filter them through their feelings before they can make up their minds. Their feelings run deep and they can be very emotional. When upset, they sulk, brood and they can even be cruel towards those who are close to them. They are extremely intuitive, they sum people up accurately, and they tend to feel everything that is going on in the surrounding atmosphere. They use this knowledge to avoid falling into traps that others simply don't see. Water sign people can be attracted to the world of business where their shrewdness and good grasp of money-matters stands them in good stead. Trust is important to them and they prefer to ally themselves to those whom they can trust and rely upon.

Water sign people can love very deeply, but some of them save their greatest love for their children or for animals. They keep sensitive feelings hidden, sometimes even from themselves, and this allows irritation and resentment to build up. Once this happens, they either fall into depression or explode - much to the surprise and hurt of those who are around them. Water sign people are restless and they like to get out and about with their work and their social life, they also love to travel and explore new places. Having said this, they also need a base, a secure home and an office, shop or workshop that they can call their own. Environments are important to them and too much noise or disturbance upsets them.

The Mutable Quality
Gemini, Virgo, Sagittarius, Pisces

Mutable signs need variety and change and this may take them into careers, which ensure that each day is different from the next. Some prefer the kind of job that takes them from one place to another, while others travel far afield. Many work in one place, but deal with a variety of people or tasks during the course of each day. Mutable sign people may choose unconventional jobs or lifestyles because it is more important for their work to fit in with their beliefs or to fulfil their spiritual needs. Many work in fields that either expand people's minds, such as writing or publishing, while others work in fields that expand their experiences, such as the travel trade or psychic work. These people sometimes choose to work in jobs that improve the lot of others, even though they can't earn much or climb the ladder of material success this way. There is a streak of independence and unconventionality about all the mutable signs, although this is less obvious in Gemini and Virgo, than it is in Sagittarius and Pisces. Many mutable sign types marry when young and start their families early. However, these early relationships all too frequently break up and they may go through a period of experimentation with a variety of partners before settling down again.

Piscean Looks

Pisceans can be tall with slightly horsy faces that feature prominent eyes and noses. Other Pisceans are of average height and with a slightly chubby appearance, pale eyes and slightly "fluffy" hair. Most have a ready smile. Many are extremely good-looking when young, but they have a tendency to retain water and to put on a lot of weight in later life and many also develop pasty and puffy faces.

Main Characteristics

Pisceans come in quite a number of varieties. Many are extraordinarily kind, gentle, vulnerable and very caring, but others can be demanding and selfish, all of which makes Pisceans quite hard to categorize. Some are reasonably businesslike while others are chaotic and apt to drift through life without ever getting their act together.

General Character

As I said in the previous paragraph, there are unpleasant Pisceans around who use their incredible intuition to sniff out those who are vulnerable, and especially to make those who work with them or under them extremely uncomfortable. Thankfully, there are far more of the other kind around, so having got this out of the way, I would now like to focus on the vast majority of Pisceans who shudder at the thought of causing pain to anybody.

Pisceans are highly intelligent and extremely intuitive. Many are psychic. These subjects care deeply about those who they love and they often take on responsibility for looking after those who find it hard to look after themselves. This takes them into the caring professions or makes them a kind of earth mother, or family daddy who looks after all the younger children in the family, often including their own grandchildren. These people make the most loyal and caring friends and they never let a friend down if they can help it. Some work for charities and they can go out of their way to look after the poorest people in their own or somebody else's society.

These people have the softest hearts. It goes without saying that they will also save animals, the planet and anything else that they can find to rescue. I know one Pisces lady who rescues pot plants that have been badly treated. These subjects are emotional and extremely vulnerable, and some are too ready to trust and believe in those who they like.

Many Pisceans find their way into the mind, body and spirit fields, and they can be found working as healers, mediums, crystal gazers, witches, clairvoyants, Tarot readers and alternative therapists of all kinds. Some of them understand astrology, palmistry, numerology and the Kabbala, but they are usually more attuned to the less structured and more mystical arts. Others are extremely religious. The quest is identical, whichever way it manifests itself. The aim is to understand heaven's mysteries and to feel connected to the "other side" and to a world that is not obvious to the five senses. Their active imagination quickly takes them into a world of unicorns and anthropomorphic dolphins. Like their next-door-neighbors, the Aquarians, some Pisceans live with their heads in the clouds and their feet miles off the ground, but while the Aquarian is trying to figure out quantum physics and how things work in a physical way, the Piscean is trying to grasp concepts and realities that can't be grasped.

Some Pisceans lead chaotic lives, never really getting their act together. Some can hold down a job but can't cope with relationships. Piscean men can make life difficult for the women who fall in love with them. They are truly sympathetic, gentle, sensitive and caring, and they can be excellent listeners, which is very attractive to a sensitive, vulnerable woman or one who is at a difficult point in her life. However, they are not strong enough to carry others, however much they want to, so inevitably they end up disappointing those who wish to rely on them or to batten on to them.

These people are not terribly ambitious and they don't have the energy to become captains of industry, but curiously enough, they don't much like it when others climb the ladder of success and leave them behind. Some Pisceans are too footloose to settle anywhere, and they drift, hippie-like, from place to place and person to person. Some escape reality through alcoholism or drugs; others use talents such as music, drama and dance to take them into another world. Most Pisceans are talented and their artistic and creative talents can take them into almost any direction. Whatever they do with their lives, they need a creative outlet. I have known Pisceans who have created a wonderful home out of a wreck, built classic cars out of bits and pieces, painters, musicians, dancers, singers and mystics and psychics of all kinds.

Pisces Careers

Vast numbers of Pisceans work in the mind, body and spirit fields and the same goes for many other Sun sign people who happen to have their Moon in Pisces. I once remember working on a stand at a psychic festival with a dozen or so consultants, and every one of us had the Sun or Moon in Pisces - or both. Many work in areas where they can do something for the community in general, such as religious ministers, charity workers and all forms of care work and in teaching. Pisceans will work in children's homes, homes for the elderly, mental health institutions, social services as prison visitors and in many other such fields. In a less obvious way, they work for the community in small post offices, small shops and in areas such as mending or recycling things. This includes thrift or charity shops, restoring china or furniture or recycling used goods. Many serve the public by working as hairdressers, by serving food or looking after hotel or bed and breakfast guests. Many find their way into the entertainment business and others look after animals. Some write fairy stories or wonderful, magical music.

As you can see, there are many avenues, but all Pisceans need personal fulfillment from their work and the feeling that they are doing something useful, and that they are doing God's work.

Money - What Money?

Piscean values are spiritual rather than material so making lots of money doesn't enter into it for most of them. It is far more important for them to do something meaningful with their lives than to earn large sums. If they do acquire money, they are likely to let it drift away or to spend it on other family members. Piscean people are workers, and they often work extremely hard in jobs that pay very little. Some are practical and careful, but they seem to have a strange karma that removes money from them despite all their efforts to hang on to it. Many are amazingly tight-fisted and stingy, especially over small matters. Some live carefully, almost frugally, and then spend large sums on drink or on silly things that they simply can't live without. Some hate to be indebted, others don't even notice. Some live off the goodwill of other people, others collect lame ducks who live off them. It is difficult to do business with these people or to deal with them, because it is impossible to know what their values are and where they are coming from.

Home Life

This being the peculiar and chaotic sign that it is, one would imagine that Pisces homes would be disorganized dumps. They're not. Pisceans are surprisingly domestic and they usually have very nice homes. The home may not be large, but it will be nicely decorated and furnished. They are surprisingly good at decorating and do-it-yourself, so if they can't afford to get jobs done, they learn how to do them for themselves. Their homes are often full of relatives, friends and passers-by, but they are very rarely dirty or disorganized. This seems to be the one area where the average Piscean has his or her act together. Pisceans are great cooks and they love to entertain. They usually have green fingers and thumbs, as they love gardening and especially growing vegetables, fruit and herbs. Many Pisceans move house several times during their lives, and they have a knack for making almost anything habitable. I have even known some who choose to live in a recreational vehicle of some kind - or a tent.

Relationships

There are no hard and fast rules here. Some Pisceans have conventional marriages; many do not. Some never leave their parents or settle down with a sister or brother. Some live in nonsexual relationships with friends. Many marry more than once and some marry many times. Some will move on from a partner, live with several others and then go back to an earlier one. Some are traditional; others are not. This is a surprisingly sexual sign and this can lead them into a number of strange relationships, which may never really come to anything. Some prefer drifting to permanence. These people usually maintain reasonably good relationships with their parents, other relatives and their children, even if they drift away physically from them. Many Pisceans end up caring fully or partly for their grandchildren.

Health

Pisceans are a pretty healthy lot on the whole and they often live long lives. They can suffer from water retention, rheumatics and high blood pressure. Most have poor eyesight or eyes that are sensitive to light or dryness. Some have really bad feet. Others give themselves problems due to smoking, drinking or drug taking.

A Few Stray Facts

Pisceans are hard to categorize, but most are very sociable and the nicest and most sympathetic friends a person can have.

Many Pisceans are emotional and vulnerable, which means that they can be subject to depression and deep unhappiness.

Pisceans can fall in love at the drop of a hat and their feelings are so strong that they can be overwhelming.

They adore the sea and they like to live near water.

Pisceans love to travel and to live among different races and types of people. They are broad-minded and don't make judgements about people by race, religion, wealth, sexual orientation or anything else.

Many of these subjects live in a land of imagination and dreams, never really getting to grips with reality. Others are perfectly realistic, but they attach themselves to partners who are chaotic and who make their lives impossible.

Pisceans are excellent swimmers and many are also very good at sports. Dancing and music come easily to this sign and most love to dance.

These people are extremely good company and they simply love to dress up, go out and have a great time and a good laugh.

The Piscean sense of humor is absolutely wonderful.

Pisces Decans

The first Decan is also Pisces, but the second is Cancer and the third is Scorpio. Read through the brief descriptions below and then turn to the chapters on Cancer and Scorpio.

1st Decan, Pisces

This emphasizes all the Piscean character traits and makes for emotional and vulnerable characters. These subjects can be disorganized in financial matters. These Pisceans usually seek out work in a caring profession or they take on the care of relatives or animals. Many are extremely psychic, artistic and musical.

2nd Decan, Cancer

The Cancer influence brings a little common sense to the sign and it also helps them to create a more normal kind of family life. These Pisceans are excellent cooks, carpenters, do-it-yourself experts and homemakers, and they are usually less silly over financial matters than the other two kinds. They may be interested in history or in collecting things that have a history attached to them. Some are extremely moody and difficult at times.

3rd Decan, Scorpio

The Scorpio influence aids the intuitive faculties and makes these Pisceans very quick to see through other people. They may be somewhat manipulative, using others for their own ends. These Pisceans can be quite ambitious, but they are often as ambitious for their children or even their partner as for themselves. They love animals and may actually like these better than they do people. These Pisceans can be excellent artists or craft workers. Oddly enough, the martial Scorpio influence takes many of these Pisceans into the armed forces, especially the navy. Others do extremely well in politics, where their combination of idealism, ambition and ability to tap into and to express what the public want, take them far.

Pisces Dwaads

The first Dwaad is also Pisces, so no change here. For all other Dwaads, read the chapter on the sign in question and also the brief descriptions given below to see what adjustments are made to the original sign.

Sign	What is added
Pisces	Pure Pisces.
Aries	Action, adventurousness, more ability, less chaos and a sharp tongue.
Taurus	Practicality, the ability to finish what is started, a talent for art and music.
Gemini	Intelligence, friendliness, an interest in business, restlessness.
Cancer	Love of home, family and pets. Common sense and financial sense.
Leo	Friendliness, love of drama, desire to be center stage, deviousness.
Virgo	Intelligence, self-sacrifice, an interest in health and healing.
Libra	Sexuality, attractiveness, talent for arbitration, artistry.
Scorpio	Intuition, psychism, sexiness. Can be over-emotional or manipulative.
Sagittarius	Love of travel and freedom, interest in new and different people.
Capricorn	Business sense, the ability to combine caring work with achievement.
Aquarius	Ingenuity, logic, intellect. This person is a true original.

The Rising Sign

Nowadays, many people know what sign they have rising, and most of them are also aware that the term "Ascendant" means the same thing. To be precise, the rising sign is the sign of the zodiac that was coming up over the eastern horizon at a person's time of birth, while the Ascendant is the exact degree of that sign. Obviously this Ascendant will fall into a specific Decan and a Dwaad, and this will make the childhood experiences and some aspects of the person's nature quite unlike others who were born with the same sign rising.

There are many books on the market that deal with rising signs; my own book is now part of a compendium called "How to Read Your Star Signs". Therefore, if you treat yourself to a book or two on this subject, and then once you have worked out which sign, Decan and Dwaad you are dealing with on your own chart and on those of others, you can easily check these out by reading the story for each feature, treating each component part as a rising sign in its own right and then reading the relevant chapter.

For example, a person with Gemini rising could have a Gemini, Libra or Aquarius Decan and a Dwaad from any one of the twelve zodiac signs on the actual ascendant degree. This person would need to read the chapter on Gemini as a rising sign, but also Libra or Aquarius, if those Decans happen to subrule the sign, and then they could check out the situation for whatever Dwaad sign is in operation.

Until you find the books you need, here is a summary that will give you something to work with.

Aries as a Rising sign, Decan or Dwaad

One or even both parents may be domineering and unreasonable; confrontations are particularly likely to occur when the child reaches his teens, and then he or she may escape by leaving home when young, in order to get away from the parental pressure. Some Aries rising subjects will go into the armed forces to get away, while others marry and start a family while very young. Others will simply take off and establish a separate life from that of the parents. Choosing to leave or to stay and fight depends upon the person's basic nature and on many factors in his horoscope. Often this subject is the oldest child in the family, one who doesn't quite fit in at home, or the one who somehow seems to set off peevish or domineering behavior from the parent in question. This person may be naturally rather self-centered, or he may develop a level of selfishness out of sheer self-preservation. The Aries rising person is usually of medium height, with a pale skin and ordinary looks.

Taurus as a rising sign, Decan or Dwaad

In theory this should be a pleasant sign to have around, but so often something is askew in the subject's childhood. The childhood experiences make financial security or financial independence an imperative. Sometimes the child learns from his parents that a large and well-appointed house, lots of possessions and status symbols, along with plenty of money in the bank are the keys to a happy life. This means that he chases after these things throughout adulthood either by working for them or perhaps as a result of marriage. However, Taurus around the ascendant adds a practical streak along with creative talent and sociability, which being allied to a good head for money matters endows this person a great opportunity for worldly success. This is all well and good, but some who have this sign rising don't make it, and that makes them bitter. For some inexplicable reason, there are some who have this sign rising who are selfish, argumentative and unpleasant to be around. The Taurus rising subject may be quite slim, but they have a slight look of a bulldog about their mouths.

Gemini as a rising sign, Decan or Dwaad

I call this the sign of the orphan, because even if the child is not partially or wholly orphaned, they often feel like it. This rising sign denotes loneliness and difficulty in childhood, even if there are people around, the child will feel alone or misunderstood. Even if the home life was good, this person would have felt alienated at school or elsewhere. Gemini rising children are friendly relaters and they lack the kind of caution that distances them from hurtful people or situations. They blame themselves when others behave badly to them, being sure that it must be something that they are doing that causes them to deserve or attract the pain that they suffer.

This child is talkative, and while our adult world welcomes communicators, schoolteachers frequently try to shut them up. However, the parents do all they can to stimulate the child's intellect. Adults with Gemini rising can be cutting and far too quick to express an opinion, but usually only when they are being badly treated. Later in life, some of these subjects choose to marry partners who appear strong and confident because they think that they will look after them. In some cases, this works, in others it doesn't. Unless they can find the right outlet for their intelligence and talents, they continue to feel like a square peg in a round hole at work as well as at home. The Gemini rising child may be an only child, an unwanted child or a late addition to parents who thought that they had completed their family and who are bored with the thought of bringing up yet another child. They may start out being wanted, only to become an encumbrance or embarrassment to their parent or parents later on. The Gemini rising person is very thin when young, slim during mid-life, but they can become quite plump later on, and they sometimes have rather fine hair.

Cancer as a rising sign, Decan or Dwaad

This can be an excellent rising sign or a surprisingly difficult one. The mother is a strong influence and often a strong role model. In some cases, the child's mother is deeply loving, but in others she is a powerful and frightening figure. The Cancer rising child is often the older one who either takes or is given the responsibility for looking after the younger members of the family. This person may go on later to marry a younger partner or one who is, sick, insecure or who needs mothering or shoring up. The Cancer rising nature is cautious and sometimes quite suspicious of others. These people are deeply intuitive and they only deal with those who they can trust. Most have good business heads on their shoulders and they are capable and responsible with money and with other aspects of their lives. One fault that seems to beset some of these people is that of penny-pinching stinginess or a talent for spending large sums on one thing and being far too thrifty on others. As children, they sit at the back of the classroom and try to keep out of everyone's way. Some endure school and get out as soon as they can; others do quite well at school. The Cancer rising person is usually nice looking with a rounded face and figure. They often have plenty of slightly wavy hair.

Leo as a rising sign, Decan or Dwaad

This suggests that the child was wanted, but he may turn out to be such a handful that the parents switch off from him or become tired of his company. In many cases, the child is extremely talented and also good-looking and the parents may push him to achieve great success, often in some artistic or show-business field. There is no rule as to the child's position in a family, but he will certainly stand out in some way. He may be the only boy in a family of girls or vice versa, or the only one with artistic, musical or creative talent in a rather ordinary family. The adult with this rising sign may suffer from the feeling that he didn't quite make it, that he didn't somehow reach the standard that was expected of him. These people can be self-centered and they can go through life as though they are acting a part rather than living in the real world. They can go on the attack when faced with people who they deem to be more successful than themselves, and they can be defensive and hurtful when there is nothing to defend and nobody setting out to hurt them. As school children, these subjects can do very well or very badly, but they usually have some kind of talent that marks them out as being "special". Leo rising people are good-looking and sometimes rather vain.

Virgo as a rising sign, Decan or Dwaad

This difficult sign suggests that there was something wrong during childhood. Even when he or she is wanted in the first place, somehow fate soon decrees that he gets in somebody's way. Sometimes the mother simply can't cope, is sickly or neurotic. The parents (especially the mother) are in some way detached or distanced from the child. This may be due to circumstances or due to the fact that the parents find something more interesting to do than to bring up a child. These children can be fussy and neurotic, especially over matters related to health or food and they can become hypochondriacs. The child is clever, but he may be shy or backward in coming forward in some way. Sometimes this child simply doesn't gel with the rest of the family. In other cases his loud voice and fondness for speaking out irritates schoolteachers, who spend years trying to shut him up. The adult world embraces communicators, but schoolteachers loathe them. Virgo rising people do better in later life when their ability to sort, analyze and investigate matters, and their habit of reading and studying deeply stand them in good stead. These subjects can be confrontational, argumentative and cutting when they feel the need to defend themselves. These people often have pale skins, a good bone structure and dark hair, and they keep their good looks throughout life as long as they don't gain too much weight.

Libra as a rising sign, Decan or Dwaad

In theory this is a pleasant feature sign to have, as the person is usually nice looking and easygoing. The reality is that the father may have been absent during childhood for much or all of the time, and the child doesn't receive the love and guidance that he needs. If the mother is angry with the father during his childhood, that gets taken on board as well. The child may be left to his own devices for much of the time or he may be spoiled with material things, toys and other goodies while missing out on true nurturing. His tendency to be lazy and to live in a dream world may make him something of a failure at school and his parents and teachers will not hesitate to point this out to him. In many cases, this type drifts easily through life. Some Libra rising subjects become bitter about the fact that society won't recognize their talents. These people are often charming, nice looking, charismatic and attractive.

Scorpio as a rising sign, Decan or Dwaad

The parents (especially the mother), are usually pretty good and the child is loved, but there are often outside circumstances that make life difficult for these children or for their families. The problem may be poverty, sickness or something else that makes them feel out of step with their peers. This breeds a cautious attitude, secrecy and deep feelings that are kept inside. These subjects develop a good deal of intuition, and they learn early to watch others and to keep their mouths shut. It takes a lot for these people to trust others or to open up to them about their true thoughts and feelings. They feel that there is more to everything than meets the eye, which may account for the large numbers of them who find their way into astrology and psychic work. Many of these subjects are only children, a different gender to their siblings or in some other way a little different from others. Scorpio rising people can descend into dreadful moods, either becoming self-pitying or giving their partners the silent punishment treatment. Scorpio rising people may be good-looking or really quite ordinary, but they have strong features and a direct gaze that is often described as "magnetic".

Sagittarius as a rising sign, Decan or Dwaad

Many astrologers and people who are interested in spiritual matters have this sign rising or in some important place on their charts. The childhood seems to be reasonable, but the child is keen to leave home early and to experiment with different ideas from those that his parents and schoolteachers had tried to force upon him. If the child is brought up in a strongly religious atmosphere, he will almost inevitably reject this and look for meaning in other philosophies. This rising sign often belongs to a quite favored younger child in the family who gets away with murder. Alternatively, this is the kind of child who makes friends with some other family and almost moves in on them or in some other way finds reasons to spend as little time at home as possible. These people are kind, humorous and sympathetic, but they can be tactless and extremely sarcastic, competitive and hurtful when they feel the need. These people are fairly tall and often quite plain in appearance with a long jaw or a horsy face. Their friendly, humorous and intelligent natures make them popular.

Capricorn as a rising sign, Decan or Dwaad

This signifies a hard childhood, but this is not necessarily due to bad parents or bad parenting. Sometimes there are many brothers and sisters in the family, and in other cases poverty is a factor. The child learns early that money in the bank, a fully paid up house, security and a decent career are important. He may be hard working and serious at a time when other youngsters are having fun. He takes life seriously and he may feel that he lacks something that other children have. In some cases the Capricorn rising child is sickly, in others he misses out on schooling. One saving grace for these children is that they often form excellent relationships with their grandparents, and they therefore become more comfortable in the presence of older people than they do with those of their own age. Their lack of confidence and sometimes-painful shyness means that they find personal relationships difficult, although if they find the right partner later in life, they make excellent relationships with all members of their families. These people can be clannish, selfish and unable to acknowledge the needs and feelings of others. These people can look old when they are young and young when they are old and their looks improve with age.

Aquarius as a rising sign, Decan or Dwaad

Aquarius rising people may have an unusual character or an unusual way of looking at life. They learn to be independent early on, either because they have to stand on their own two feet or because their parents encourage them to do so. The childhood is usually pretty good, although there may be a level of instability that means that the child attends several different schools or lives in a variety of different places. The parents do all they can to ensure that the child receives a good education and plenty of mental stimulation. These subjects cannot swallow the opinions of others whole because they need to think things through and make up their own mind. They have a pleasant manner that endears them to others and they have no trouble making new friends. They usually get on well in family life, as long as they don't end up with a partner who seeks to control them. These subjects keep their thoughts and feelings to themselves, but they often feel contempt for those around them. If necessary, they will cut off completely from those who have hurt them. At school they are not particularly successful in academic subjects, but they do well with technical topics. Some take to computing, others to motor mechanics or engineering. Others are successful at sports. These people are taller than average and rather nice looking, and they remain pretty good to look at throughout life.

Pisces as a rising sign, Decan or Dwaad

There is often an element of loneliness in this person's childhood, even if there are many brothers and sisters in the family. Sometimes this is due to spells in hospital; sometimes it is the result of circumstances beyond anyone's control. The parents do their best, but they are often ineffective, so the child learns to cope by himself. Despite the fact that the sign of Pisces is not associated with career or business success, this person often does rather well in life. The problem is that he may waste the gains that he makes by propping up a needy partner later in life. Pisces rising subjects usually have a prickly and hostile manner that makes them uncomfortable to be with. Perhaps this is some kind of defense mechanism that grows out of having to keep others at a distance when they are young, or perhaps the roots are some kind of inferiority complex. These people are at their happiest when they develop their artistic, musical, creative or psychic talents, and once they achieve some success and their self-confidence develops, they become nicer to be with. These people tend to be pale skinned, fair haired and their looks are pleasantly ordinary.

The Moon Sign

The Moon sign shows how you react to situations, it also shows habitual behavior and the way you act and feel when you are sick, depressed or even when slightly drunk. It shows your inner, emotional nature. This also offers information about how well you were loved and nurtured in childhood and how you nurture others in turn. The Moon sign will indicate the kind of home you choose, whether you like traveling, whether you seek a conventional form of family life or something different. The Moon placement can show whether you will work with or for the public or not.

The Moon is bound to be influenced by the sign it falls into, by its Decan and to a lesser extent, its Dwaad. Two people with the same Moon sign will have much in common on an emotional level, but if the Decans and Dwaads are different, their emotional needs, responses to situations, their domestic life, inner urges and their childhood experiences will be slightly different. If you happen to know the degree of your Moon sign, you can get some idea of what is going on by reading through the relevant Sun sign section of this book, although you need to bear in mind that the Moon sign is somewhat different and far less obvious to others than your Sun sign.

The following is a very brief indication of the way a Decan or Dwaad may affect your Moon, whatever sign it happens to be in.

Sign	What is added by the Decan or Dwaad
Aries	Strength and a competitive spirit, difficult father. Prefers work to home.
Taurus	Needs financial and emotional security and a nice home.
Gemini	Friendly attitude, but only real attachments being with the family.
Cancer	Teaching ability, love for partner, home and family. May travel.
Leo	Pride, high standards, may push children to succeed. Affection.
Virgo	Difficult relationship with mother. Mother may be sick or crazy.
Libra	Desire for nice things and love of beauty, thus high earner. Sexuality.
Scorpio	Sexuality, deep emotions and deep resentments. Successful worker.
Sagittarius	Humor, love of travel, craftsmanship, interest in spiritual matters.
Capricorn	Desires financial and emotional security. Inner loneliness, outer strength.
Aquarius	Independence, lack of interest in the opinions of others.
Pisces	Self-centeredness, love of travel, interest in spiritual matters.

Planetary Connections

You will notice that a particular planet rules each Sun sign.
For the sake of convenience, astrologers also call the Sun and Moon
planets. Before the invention of the telescope, Mercury, Venus, Mars,
Jupiter and Saturn could be seen by the naked eye, so these, (along
with the Sun and Moon), were the rulers of the zodiac signs. Each
planet ruled two signs, apart from the Sun and Moon, which had
one each to themselves. In time, Uranus, Neptune and Pluto took
over some of the signs, and now Chiron may be posed to take over
yet another. Here are both the modern and ancient planetary rulers.

Sign	Modern Rulers	Ancient Rulers
Aries	Mars	Mars
Taurus	Venus	Venus
Gemini	Mercury	Mercury
Cancer	Moon	Moon
Leo	Sun	Sun
Virgo	Mercury/Chiron	Mercury
Libra	Venus	Venus
Scorpio	Pluto	Mars
Sagittarius	Jupiter	Jupiter
Capricorn	Saturn	Saturn
Aquarius	Uranus	Saturn
Pisces	Neptune	Jupiter

The Planets and the Decans & Dwaads

Just as a planet rules each sign, so does it rule each Decan and Dwaad. The following very brief explanation will give you some idea of the energies of each of the planets, but if you want more information, it would be best to invest in several good books on planets and astrology, to take a course, join an astrology group, to buy astrology software and to search the Internet for information.

Aries

Mars was the ancient Roman god of war, hence the assertive and martial nature that is added to any sign when an Aries Decan or Dwaad is in operation. Sometimes this adds an idealistic touch or an interest in politics.

Taurus

The lovely goddess of love, values and valuables adds possessiveness, materialism, laziness, artistry a love of luxury and beauty to any Taurus Decan or Dwaad.

Gemini

The messenger planet, Mercury, adds a search for knowledge, a need for variety and the ability to communicate, write or get around the neighborhood to any Gemini Decan or Dwaad.

Cancer

The emotional Moon adds feeling, intuition and love for home and family to any Cancer Decan or Dwaad. Also common sense and caution, especially with regard to money matters.

Leo

The regal Sun adds a touch of grandeur, high standards and a tendency towards arrogance to any Leo Decan or Dwaad. Sometimes charisma and a love of drama occur.

Virgo
The fussy, medically minded, methodical Mercury adds an interest in health, analysis, order and a desire to work hard to any Virgo Decan or Dwaad. This can add a touch of neurosis.

Libra
The beauteous love planet, Venus, adds mystique and feminine charisma as well as indecisiveness and sexiness to any Libra Decan or Dwaad. This can make the person somewhat unrealistic.

Scorpio
The investigative nature of Mars or Pluto adds intrigue, secretiveness, tenacity and determination to any Scorpio Decan or Dwaad. It can also add resentment or a touch of cruelty.

Sagittarius
Jupiter, the seeker after justice adds fairness, broad-mindedness, honesty, spirituality and an interest in legal matters, education and travel to any Sagittarian Decan or Dwaad.

Capricorn
Businesslike Saturn adds common sense, ambition and a capacity for dealing with details to any Capricorn Decan or Dwaad. It can have a dampening or depressing influence.

Aquarius
The organized but unusual Saturn or Uranus adds an excellent intellect and an inventive mentality to any Aquarius Decan or Dwaad. This also adds a touch of eccentricity.

Pisces
The mystical Jupiter or Neptune adds spirituality and compassion to any Pisces Decan or Dwaad. This can add a touch of chaos or disorganization.

Predicting the Future

For Absolute Beginners

There are a variety of techniques used by astrologers who wish to predict events. Most require more knowledge than a beginner has to hand, but one extremely simple method that an absolute beginner can do is to "progress" the Sun. You can choose to look at the year you are in right now, or indeed, any year of your life, past or future. The basis of the method is to count as many days forward as the years you require. For example, if you want to look at the picture during your thirtieth year of life, you count forward thirty days.

N.B.: Take great care! Read and follow the simple instructions below, because if you go at this too quickly, you may end up looking at the wrong year. You will see what I mean when you look through the instructions.

How to Progress Your Sun

1. Write down your age at present
2. Use the calendar that follows these instructions to count forward one day for each year of your life. I suggest that you definitely use the calendar for this rather than trying to work it out in your head, because you can easily end up one day short of the one you need. Look at the following example to see what I mean.

John Doe was born on June 1 and he is now 28 years old. Logic says that his "progressed Sun date" will be June 28, but this is not so. If John was born on the 1st, he was one year old on the 2nd, two years old on the 3rd and so forth, ending up at the age of 28 on *June 29!* Check this by counting forwards 28 days using the calendar below to see this for yourself.

Calendar for the month of June						
1	2	3	4	5	6	7
8	9	10	11	12	13	14
15	16	17	18	19	20	21
22	23	24	25	26	27	28
29	30					

Once you have discovered your ***progressed*** birth date, go back and look it up on the Decan and Dwaad calendar in exactly the same way as you did for your original date of birth to find the Decan and Dwaad for your progressed Sun.

Bear in mind that your life will be somewhat easier whenever the Sun is in a Decan or Dwaad that shares the same element as the sign that it was in when you were born. Another easy scenario is a combination of fire/air, or earth/water but other combinations are hard to live through. I have a Leo friend who has lived through some tough times in recent years, but her Sun has just crossed into the Gemini Decan and Gemini Dwaad of Libra, which should make her life easier. Time will tell if this is so.

While you are busy counting, remember that some years are leap years. If the person you are looking into has a birthday that occurs in January or February and progressing the Sun takes it from

February into March, you will need to know whether the person's year of birth was a leap year. Check the dates in the following table.

Leap Years

1900	1904	1908	1912	1916	1920	1924	1928
1932	1936	1940	1944	1948	1952	1956	1960
1964	1968	1972	1976	1980	1984	1988	1992
1996	2000	2004	2008	2012	2016	2020	2024

Next, find your own birthday in the calendars on the following pages, and start counting...

Calendar for the month of January

1	2	3	4	5	6	7
8	9	10	11	12	13	14
15	16	17	18	19	20	21
22	23	24	25	26	27	28
29	30	31				

Calendar for the month of February

1	2	3	4	5	6	7
8	9	10	11	12	13	14
15	16	17	18	19	20	21
22	23	24	25	26	27	28
(29)						

Calendar for the month of March

1	2	3	4	5	6	7
8	9	10	11	12	13	14
15	16	17	18	19	20	21
22	23	24	25	26	27	28
29	30	31				

Calendar for the month of April

1	2	3	4	5	6	7
8	9	10	11	12	13	14
15	16	17	18	19	20	21
22	23	24	25	26	27	28
29	30					

Calendar for the month of May

1	2	3	4	5	6	7
8	9	10	11	12	13	14
15	16	17	18	19	20	21
22	23	24	25	26	27	28
29	30	31				

Calendar for the month of June

1	2	3	4	5	6	7
8	9	10	11	12	13	14
15	16	17	18	19	20	21
22	23	24	25	26	27	28
29	30					

Calendar for the month of July

1	2	3	4	5	6	7
8	9	10	11	12	13	14
15	16	17	18	19	20	21
22	23	24	25	26	27	28
29	30	31				

Calendar for the month of August

1	2	3	4	5	6	7
8	9	10	11	12	13	14
15	16	17	18	19	20	21
22	23	24	25	26	27	28
29	30	31				

Calendar for the month of September

1	2	3	4	5	6	7
8	9	10	11	12	13	14
15	16	17	18	19	20	21
22	23	24	25	26	27	28
29	30					

Calendar for the month of October

1	2	3	4	5	6	7
8	9	10	11	12	13	14
15	16	17	18	19	20	21
22	23	24	25	26	27	28
29	30	30				

Calendar for the month of November

1	2	3	4	5	6	7
8	9	10	11	12	13	14
15	16	17	18	19	20	21
22	23	24	25	26	27	28
29	30					

Calendar for the month of December

1	2	3	4	5	6	7
8	9	10	11	12	13	14
15	16	17	18	19	20	21
22	23	24	25	26	27	28
29	30	31				

Now you can move forward to the part of this chapter that tells you what the year you are looking into will bring.

For Student Astrologers

Using degrees will give more accuracy than the simple date system outlined above and you can progress your Sun by the simple expedient of moving it one degree for each year of life. Thus, if you are 38 years of age, count 38 degrees forward and check the new position.

Once you have experimented with your progressed Sun, you can do the same for the Moon, ascendant, Midheaven or any other feature on your chart. The progressed Moon is especially interesting, as it is the trigger for so much that goes on in our lives. The easiest way to do this is with astrology software, but if you want to check out the progressed Moon by hand, this is how you do it.

Finding the Progressed Moon

Check out the natal Moon's position on your date of birth against the one that is shown in your ephemeris. Unless you were born at exactly the same time as that given in your ephemeris, you will notice a discrepancy of several degrees either way. Take a note of this difference. Now count forward in the ephemeris as many days as the years of your life. Do this carefully so that you end up at the right year. Finally, make exactly the same adjustment for the progressed Moon as for your natal Moon position.

For example, if your Ephemeris tells you that your natal Moon was at 20 deg. Sagittarius, but you know that it was actually 24 deg. Sagittarius, add four degrees to that which is given in the ephemeris. The same goes for a Moon position that is a few degrees less than that given in the ephemeris. This method will show you the position of the progressed Moon on your actual birth month. Now, if you want to look at the position a few months after your month of birth, count forward one degree for every month following your month of birth. For example, if you were born in January, but you want to look at the situation in September, add eight degrees to the adjusted progressed Moon's position.

Once you have found the new position, check it out on the Decan and Dwaad calendar to see which Decan and Dwaads are in operation for the month that you wish to look into.

Some people enjoy doing hand calculations while others hate them, if you can't stand the idea of fiddling around with the ephemeris, treat yourself to some decent software or look at the Internet, because there are downloadable free chart services and much more available on there, and it is increasing all the time.

If you have managed to progress your Moon, you can use the information given below to see what is happening on a monthly basis. The Moon tends to work on an inner, emotional level rather than taking action in the way that the Sun does, but it acts as such a trigger for our own actions and the things that are thrown at us, so the readings given below will still be relevant.

The interpretations below can also be used for any planet, angle or feature on a chart, but remember to synthesize the energy of the planet or feature in question with that of the sign, Decan and Dwaad. This is a lot to remember, but it works. Remember that each Decan and Dwaad is also related to the energies of the planets that rule the zodiac sign in question. Thus, if your progressed Venus (money, values, luxury) is in the Pisces Dwaad and Sagittarius Decan of the sign of Aries, you have all these energies to take into account.

Interpreting the Progressed Decans and Dwaads

In this section, I have tried to show the kind of energy that each sign gives to the Sun or to any other planet or feature that arrives there. The twelve interpretations below should be applied to any sign, Decan or Dwaad that you wish to look into. Remember to combine the factors. For example, if your Sun has progressed to the Scorpio Decan of Pisces, you will need to read both Pisces and Scorpio. If you then discover that it is in the Libran Dwaad, you will need to read Libra as well.

It takes the Sun thirty years to move through a sign, ten years to move through a Decan and two or three years to move through a Dwaad, so a combination of factors will need to be taken into account during any one year. For instance, my own Sun has now progressed to the cusp of the Gemini Decan and Gemini Dwaad of Libra. This means that my progressed Sun has been traveling through Libra for 20 years, through the Aquarian Decan for ten years and through the Taurus Dwaad for a couple of years or so. Now things are on the point of changing.

Aries

This progression brings a time of fresh starts and an increase of ambition and activity. The subject will not allow the grass to grow under his feet at this time because he will grasp the opportunities that rush towards him. He must guard against impatience and arrogance, because he won't be able to cope with fools or those who think and act slowly. The person may become more idealistic, which may lead him to take up cudgels for a cause that grabs his attention. When the Moon progresses to Aries, a house move is sometimes on the cards.

Taurus

The subject might become somewhat dogmatic and opinionated, but he will also be able to achieve a great deal. The main benefit is that the subject's financial position will improve and he will be able to save for the future. A more cautious attitude will prevail and there will be considerable success in business due to increased shrewdness. He may become interested in art, music or improving his home and garden and making them more attractive. Self-esteem increases and the person is able to work out what is important to him and set out to achieve it.

Gemini

This influence increases day-to-day activity with lots of time spent on the telephone, dealing with paperwork and rushing out on local errands. Even longer distance travel is likely due to this sign's attachment to Mercury, the god who had wings on his heels. There is sometimes a stronger connection with brothers, sisters, other relatives of one's own age and also with neighbors. Teaching, learning and keeping up-to-date will be a feature of a person's life at this time. The subject may even be struck by verbal diarrhea. Health and healing may become important or interesting, as would activities that involve young people or a new interest in gadgetry and novel inventions.

Cancer

This puts the emphasis on family matters and home life. The subject may become interested in the past history of his family or in history in general, and he may start to collect antiques, coins or other objects that have past connections. Travel on or over water is possible now, as is a move of house. Issues relating to mothers and motherhood will rise to the surface now, which means that situations such as parenthood, becoming a mother-in-law, gaining a mother-in-law or looking after grandchildren could occur. The person may spend more time at home or he may take up some kind of work that he can do from home - perhaps with the help of other family members.

Leo

The progression to Leo brings a far more outgoing phase than the previous one. The subject will be more interested in the limelight than the shadows. This may manifest itself in him reaching for the top in his career or starting a business. The subject may express this by taking up amateur dramatics or a sporting activity that puts him center stage. There will be a strong desire for a creative outlet and he will feel a strong urge to make something come into existence. Sometimes babies and children come into the subject's arena, and if appropriate, he could start a family under this progression.

Virgo

In modern astrological parlance, this sign is related to work and health, while in the old days, it was said to rule servants, masters and health. The subject is likely to concentrate more on his work at this time and either takes on staff, thus becoming a master of others or he may take a job in an organization that has a hierarchy. Health is likely to become an important issue, either because the subject needs to concentrate more on his own health, or because he takes up an interest in health, healing and related subjects. Other matters might include an interest in craftwork, dressmaking, do-it-yourself jobs and such things as cooking, looking after a family and keeping pets.

Libra

This progression is concerned with relationships and connections, and it often coincides with marriage or some other open relationship, which may be personal or business - or both. There is also an increased interest in or connection with legal matters, and the subject strives for justice, either through the courts or in some other way. There will be more dealings with people and possibly also with contracts and other legal types of paperwork in connection with business. Often life gets easier, with more harmony and affection around when this progression occurs - especially if the Moon progresses to this sign.

Scorpio

Important matters that involve other people are on the cards when this progression occurs. Sometimes this involves personal relationships, such as marriage, divorce or family events that involve legal or other arrangements such as mortgages, legacies or tax matters. Sometimes there are work or business matters that involve the subject in dealings with other people and with financial matters, and this often involves looking after someone else's money, property or resources. Joint financial matters and joint arrangements will be important at this time. Serious life-changing events, such as birth, death and marriage will occur at this time.

Sagittarius

A variety of matters may come to the fore now, and all of them indicate expansion of horizons or pushing back boundaries. This can lead to travel and an interest in people or products from distant lands. Sometimes this leads the subject to question his religious or spiritual beliefs and his general philosophy of life and perhaps find something that is more meaningful to him. Higher or further education may become a factor here, as might teaching or becoming a leader in some kind of religious or spiritual field. Legal matters can become important, perhaps in the form of a fight for justice and right.

Capricorn

On one hand this is not an easy progression because life can be quite hard for a while. This is especially so when the Moon moves through this sign. The subject will work hard, sometimes alone and unappreciated and sometimes for very little in exchange. In some cases, the person has to work to get out of debt or to get back on his feet after a period of loss. The subject may feel lonely or out in the cold either due to problems in his personal life or his working life. However, the end result of the effort that is put in under this progression, is that the person eventually gets back on his feet and develops the necessary structures for a successful future. He also learns a lot about himself, others and life in general under this progression, and he may be less trusting or vulnerable to attack in the future.

Aquarius

This is the breakout sign, so a progression to this sign can bring a total change in a person's life-style. During this progression - especially if it is a lunar one - the person may move house, marry, divorce, change jobs completely or even up-sticks and emigrate. In short, anything could happen. Many people embark on a course of training or education during this progression and some find work as teachers. Others become extremely inventive or original at this time. If the subject hasn't yet got to grips with computers or other modern technology, he will need to do so now. Life will not be stable while this progression is in action, but it will not be boring either.

Pisces

This progression will make the subject more sensitive and vulnerable and his emotions are likely to become stronger, with emotional matters becoming a more important feature of his life. He may fall in love, or he may become so touched by the needs of others that he takes up some form of charitable or caring work. The chances are that he will spend more time alone, possibly working on private projects at home. Alternatively, he may become involved with hospitals or other places of seclusion, either through work or due to problems of his own. Health and healing may become a priority in some way now and the subject's psychic and imaginative powers will increase. He may become interested in artistic or musical pursuits.

Transits

Transits are the first form of predictive astrology that any astrologer learns and they are used in all newspaper and magazine horoscopes. Transits are simply the position of the Moon and planets that you can see up in the sky at any one time, but astrologers use tables to find their exact positions. This is not difficult, so student astrologers usually pick up the technique very quickly. If you know nothing about transits, the following comments won't mean anything to you, but if you are accustomed to using them they will make immediate sense.

Take any planet that you wish to examine and see what sign, Decan and Dwaad it is in and then consider the effects that this will have on it. This is probably more useful when considering the slower moving outer planets than the fast moving inner ones. For example, if you want to look at the Pluto situation in the year 2005, you will notice that it runs forward, retrograde and forward again at around 22 to 24 degrees of Sagittarius. This means that in 2005, Pluto will look like this:

Sign: Sagittarius
Decan: Leo
Dwaad: Virgo

Looking at the planetary connections, Pluto will have a Jupiter influence throughout the period due to Jupiter's rulership of the sign of Sagittarius, also a solar influence due to the Leo Decan and a Mercury influence due to the Virgo Dwaad.

Taking Things Further

If you are so far into astrology that you know which sign and house your planets occupy and the exact degree of all these, plus your descendant, Midheaven, Immum Coeli and more, you might like to work out the Decans and Dwaads of all these and see what they tell you. Checking charts for compatibility between two people is another obvious matter when it comes to Decans and Dwaads.

The Midheaven

The Midheaven will show where a person's aims and ambitions lie and what they want to make of life. This neglected area of astrology should also be studied for the effect it has on the psychology of a person, because this can show what they are really striving for. Differences in the Midheaven Dwaad typically account for the different behavior and nature between even the closest of twins, which shows just how important this is. Many people make happy relationships and partnerships with those whose Sun is in the same sign as their Midheaven, and the Decan or Dwaad will also have a bearing on this.

The Descendant

The descendant shows the kind of outlook and behavior that a person seeks from those who he chooses to like or to love. It doesn't mean that a person should marry a person whose Sun or ascendant is in the same sign as their descendant, only that they should share the values that it encompasses. Study the descendant position in full to see what it is that a person is looking for in others.

The Imum Coeli

The Imum Coeli shows the kind of background a person came from and also the kind of home and family life they would like to have. It can refer to the circumstances of the beginning and early days of a person's life, and according to tradition, this also shows the circumstances at the end of life.

Synastry

The word synastry comes from the Latin word sinister. This doesn't mean that Dracula is about to jump out of your closet, it is simply the word for left in the same way that dexter means right. In astrology, this usually refers to a lover, possibly a good friend or a business partner, thus what we are referring to here is the compatibility between two people's horoscope charts. For this, you can include the positions of the Sun, Moon, ascendant, descendant, Mars, Venus and anything else that you would like to study. If a relationship between two people is particularly good while on the face of things, their charts are not particularly compatible. In this case, take a look at the Decans and Dwaads as they may show a truer picture.

The Planets

Sometimes looking at the Decan of just one planet can tell you a great deal about the way it operates. For instance, someone with Mars or Venus in Sagittarius may be prone to chase the opposite sex if in the Sagittarius or Aries Decan, but this is far less likely to do so when in the Leo Decan. Always consider the planet that rules the Decan or Dwaad in question. For instance, a Venus ruled Dwaad will act in a different way from a Jupiter ruled one.

The Part of Fortune

The sign, house, Decan and Dwaad of the part of fortune can tell you how you will make your way in life and how you can expect to make money or make your way in the world.

The Vertex

Many people find themselves attracted to a particular type of person, sometimes in a fated or an obsessive manner, or they may find that a particular star sign turns up among their relatives, friends and lovers whether they look for this or not. Whatever the scene, study the sign, house, Decan and Dwaad of the vertex to discover what is going on.

Other Features

Absolutely anything that you choose to look into that appears on a horoscope will have its relevant Decan and Dwaad, so you can apply this to asteroids, midpoints and anything else that you fancy investigating. Try taking a look at the Black Moon, because this is a particularly destructive force on a horoscope.

A Place and Time...

Can an event that happened in a particular place and time be linked to astrology? Let us take one small area and one moment in time, and see what we can discover.

The place is Isigny, on the Vire river in Normandy, and it is close to the Omaha and Utah beachheads, where the American forces landed as part of the invasion of Normandy in the Second World War. The chart is set for H-Hour, which was just before dawn on June the 6th, 1944.

The Sun was just about to rise and cross the ascendant. The Sun symbolizes the heart of the matter - or what the allies were trying to achieve. Gemini represents brotherhood - in this case, the brotherhood of the military and of the allies. Gemini indicates youth, and most of the men involved were in their teens and early twenties. There were no hidden agendas because both the outward manifestation of the event (the ascendant) and its true meaning (the Sun) were in total agreement. Everyone knew who they were fighting, and why.

Gemini suggests that communication was of supreme importance. It had already been discovered during the practice sessions that typing errors and a lack of proper coordination could cause unnecessary deaths, but on that day, everyone involved knew what they were supposed to be doing. However, there was some lack of intelligence about the terrain and the number of German troops in the area, and there was insufficient artillery backup when it was needed.

The combination of the Sun and ascendant in the Libran Decan of Gemini suggests that this was a true partnership between the allies, and that the ultimate aim was for peace and justice. Libra is associated with open enemies.

The Sun was in the Sagittarius Dwaad, so this event took thousands of young men into a new country that had been subjected to life under a totally alien regime. The ascendant was in the Scorpio Dwaad, suggesting a fight to the death - and also something that could never be forgotten.

The Moon was in Sagittarius in its own Decan, emphasizing the need to shoot the modern equivalent of arrows at an enemy. Sagittarius rules belief systems and ideology, and here the emotional lunar motive was one of ridding the world of a dastardly ideology and replacing it with a humane and democratic one.

The Moon's Dwaad was just into Pisces, and in ancient astrology, Jupiter ruled Pisces as well as Sagittarius. The invasion reintroduced religion to a continent that was fast destroying Judaism, and Catholicism would have been next on Adolf Hitler's list.

There are other fascinating factors on this chart. Venus, the planet of open enemies, rising in conjunction with revolutionary Uranus. The warlike Mars/Pluto conjunction in Leo, close to the karmic north node of the Moon. Lastly, the Vertex in Scorpio, representing people of vital importance. Generals Montgomery, Patton and Rommel, were noted leaders in the Normandy situation. All three had the Sun in Scorpio!

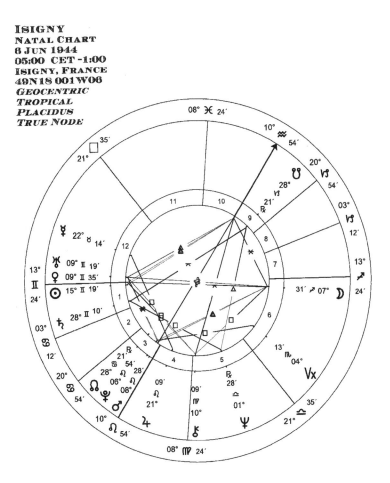

ISIGNY
NATAL CHART
6 JUN 1944
05:00 CET -1:00
ISIGNY, FRANCE
49N18 001W06
GEOCENTRIC
TROPICAL
PLACIDUS
TRUE NODE

A Few Celebrity Charts

Here are a few celebrity charts for you to check out. I have noted the birth data in full for those of you who might wish to look at the whole chart, but for the purposes of this book we will only look at the signs, Decans and Dwaads for the Sun, Moon and ascendant for each celebrity.

Venus Williams

With a name like Venus, this lady really should take up astrology! Venus is, of course, the elder of two tennis champion sisters. Although her sister, Serena, has also done extremely well, Venus seems to have the edge; and this was reinforced when the two met in a recent final and Venus was the winner. See if you can spot the reason for the older sister's greater dedication and success. Venus was born in Lynwood, CA (33N55 by 113W12) on June 17 1980 at 14:12 PDT

Sun	22 deg. 44 min. Gemini. Aquarius Decan, Aquarius Dwaad.
Moon	27 deg. 40 min. Leo. Aries Decan, Gemini Dwaad.
Asc.	13 deg. 33 min. Libra. Aquarius Decan, Pisces Dwaad.

Serena Williams

Here is Serena's data for comparison. She was born in Saginaw MI (43N25 by 83W57) on September 26 1981 at 20:28 EDT

Sun	3 deg. 49 min. Libra. Libra Decan, Scorpio Dwaad.
Moon	20 deg. 24 min. Virgo. Taurus Decan, Taurus Dwaad.
Asc.	3 deg. 10 min. Taurus. Taurus Decan, Gemini Dwaad.

MC Hammer

Rap singer MC Hammer's real name is Stanley Kirk Burrel. See if you can spot MC Hammer's love of music, originality and his way with words. He was born in Oakland CA (37N48 by 122W16) on June 30 1962 at 11:59 PST

Sun	9 deg. 38 min. Aries. Aries Decan, Cancer Dwaad.
Moon	0 deg. 44 min. Gemini. Gemini Decan, Gemini Dwaad.
Asc.	21 deg. 00 min. Cancer. Pisces Decan, Pisces Dwaad.

Angelina Jolie

Angelina Jolie played Lara Croft in the film about the computer game, Tomb Raider. See is you can spot the reason for Angelina's hard work and success in her acting career. She was born in Los Angeles (34N03 by 118W14) on June 4 1975 at 9:09 PDT

Sun	18 deg. 25 min. Gemini. Libra Decan, Capricorn Dwaad.
Moon	18 deg. 05 min. Aries. Leo Decan, Scorpio Dwaad.
Asc.	28 deg. 53 min. Cancer. Pisces Decan, Gemini Dwaad.

Oprah Winfrey

Oprah was born into a poor but respectable family, and she made the best of her quirky personality, her clever mind, her obvious idealism and her talent for communication. Oprah was born in Kosciesko MS (33N03 by 89W35) on January 29 1954 a5 4:30 CST

| Sun | 9 deg. 00 min. Aquarius. Aquarius Decan, Taurus Dwaad. |

Moon   4 deg. 32 min. Sagittarius. Sagittarius Decan, Capricorn
            Dwaad.
Asc.   29 deg. 41 min. Sagittarius. Leo Decan, Scorpio
            Dwaad.

Carlos Santana

Carlos Santana's wonderful rock music with a Latin American slant has brought pleasure to millions and he is still happily playing. A recent television interview showed him to be a real family man who is proud of his children. See if you can spot his love of music, dedication to his work and his love of family and home life. Carlos was born in Autlan De Navarro in Mexico (19N46 by 104W22) on July 20 1947 at 2:00 CST.

Sun   26 deg. 46 min. Cancer. Pisces Decan, Taurus Dwaad.
Moon   27 deg. 20 min. Leo. Aries Decan, Gemini Dwaad.
Asc.   22 deg. 07 min. Taurus. Capricorn Decan, Aquarius
            Dwaad.

Catherine Zeta Jones

Catherine Zeta Jones came from a working class Welsh family, who were all interested in acting. Spot her acting ability, her athletic prowess, her beauty and her capacity for love. Catherine Zeta Jones was born in Swansea (51N38 by 3W57) on September 25 1969 at 14:40 BST

Sun   2 deg. 18 min. Libra. Libra Decan, Libra Dwaad.
Moon   28 deg. 41 min. Pisces. Scorpio Decan, Aries Dwaad.
Asc.   22 deg. 59 min. Sagittarius. Leo Decan, Virgo Dwaad.

Celine Dion

Celine grew up in a large French Canadian family, and many of her sisters and brothers sing, but she was the one who took the talent farthest. She always talks about her family in interviews and she seems happiest when she is able to get back home and be with them. Celine Dion was born on March 30 1968 at 12.15pm EST in Charlemagne, Canada (45N43 by 73W29)

Sun	10 deg. 04 min. Aries. Leo Decan, Leo Dwaad.
Moon	29 deg. 40 min. Aries. Leo Decan, Pisces Dwaad.
Asc.	2 deg. 33 min. Leo. Leo Decan, Leo Dwaad.

Julia Roberts

By all accounts, Julia Roberts had a pretty awful childhood, although her mother did what she could to keep the family together. Her father was interested in acting and he had done some professional work way back in the past. A lucky break that brought a legacy her way, along with some help from her actor brother, Eric, got her started. Her first really big success was as Shelby in Steel Magnolias. Julia was born in Atlanta GA (33N45 by 34W23) on October 28 1967 at 0:16 EDT.

Sun	4 deg. 3 min. Scorpio. Scorpio Decan, Sagittarius Dwaad.
Moon	24 deg. 48 min. Leo. Aries Decan, Taurus Dwaad.
Asc.	27 deg. 37 min. Cancer. Pisces Decan, Taurus Dwaad.

Tiger Woods

Tiger Woods (Eldrick Tont Woods) is a world champion golfer who has won every major tournament at one time or another, including a grand slam in 2001. His father introduced him to the game as soon as he could walk, and by the time he was three years old, he was completing nine holes in less shots than many adults at his Dad's golf club. He is an extremely photogenic man with a film star smile, but when he concentrates he scowls and avoids connecting with the crowds who come to watch him. He says that this is down to the level of concentration that he needs to keep up while playing. Tiger Woods was born in Long Beach CA (33N46 by118W11) on December 30 1975 at 22:50 PST.

Sun	8 deg. 58 min. Capricorn. Capricorn Decan, Aries Dwaad.
Moon	22 deg. 23 min. Sagittarius. Leo Decan, Virgo Dwaad.
Asc.	24 deg. 25 min. Virgo. Taurus Decan, Gemini Dwaad.

Finally...

If you have a friend or relative who was born at a time that is very close to your own, check them out for the similarities and differences between yourselves. Check the Decan and Dwaad in addition to any differences in the position of their Moon or ascendant. Most of all, check the events of their lives and the timing of these, as they are likely to be very similar to and fairly close in time to your own. I have met a number of women whose birth data were very close to my own, and in each case the major events and circumstances of our lives have been extraordinarily similar, but the differences in Dwaad positions definitely made slight variations.

Index